Layout & Design by: Amy Van Hoosier

by
Marvin and Joy Gibson

Photography by
Marvin Gibson

Published by
L-W Book Sales
P.O. Box 69
Gas City, IN 46933

ISBN# 0-89538-059-5

Table of Contents

Dedication

This book is dedicated in loving memory to my daughter, Sherri, who died in 1983 at the age of 20 from melanoma cancer. The course of my life changed direction at that time, which led me to meeting my husband, Marvin, and writing this book with him.

The Pricing

Acknowledgments

First of all, we wish to thank L-W BOOK SALES for accepting our manuscript. It's great that they will take a chance on unknown authors.

We would also like to thank Pat and Joe Fay of Jamestown, Missouri for all the time they spent entering our information into their computer and doing all the rewrites until we were satisfied. We could never have done this without them.

Thanks to Ann and Jerry McClain of Higginsville, Missouri for taking pictures of their private collection of Roseville, Weller and Hull wall pockets and making them available to us.

Doris and Burdell Hall of Morton, Illinois were so helpful with identifying our Morton wall pockets. Without their help we would not have had a Morton chapter. Burdell worked for MORTON POTTERY COMPANY and he and Doris wrote a book on Morton's Potteries: MORTON'S POTTERIES: 99 YEARS.

Lois Crouch of Colorado Springs, Colorado was so nice and helpful when we called her asking about Van Briggle pottery. She wrote a book on the early works of Artus and Anne Van Briggle.

Wendy Winters of Eldon, Missouri for working so hard to get the pictures developed just right. She went beyond what we asked for. Good job, Wendy!

John and Shorty at Josh's Antiques in Sunrise Beach, Missouri for all their help with our research and always being so helpful when we go in.

And a special thanks to Lana and Kenneth Moore of Springfield, Missouri (Joy's sister) for always being on the look-out for wall pockets and either buying them or calling us to let us know where they are.

Our friends Norman and Esther Gunnink, and Garold and Mary Jane Vestweber of Boone, Iowa for saving every wall pocket they find, for our inspection.

And last, but certainly not least, our thanks to Rhonda Gerken of Sedalia, Missouri. She gave us the name for our book when it was just an idea in our minds. Now it's a reality.

And to all the people, everywhere we have gone, for answering all the questions we asked, or for steering us in the right direction to find our answers. Thank you all!

INTRODUCTION

When Marvin and I were married in 1987, he had been involved with flea markets and antiques for many years. I had been to one flea market before meeting him. He really initiated me into the business. Fast! It only took one time of going with him to sell some of the "junk" he had collected to hook me. I really liked getting money for something that I thought no one would want.

We have continued going to flea markets, auctions, and garage sales for the past six years, buying, selling and collecting one thing or another. But after getting a wall pocket in a box at an auction in Des Moines, Iowa in 1987, I fell in love with them. It was a clock with a bird sitting on top. The birds tail had been broken and glued back on. Badly at that! But I thought it was so cute that I hung it on our kitchen wall. That one has turned into over 1500 now, and my love for wall pockets is still as strong as ever.

Marvin indulged me in my quest for more wall pockets, until about two years ago. Then he suddenly found that he was having more fun looking for wall pockets than for the things he collected. So, we are now collecting wall pockets together and we travel around the country when we can, hoping to find one that we don't have.

We have seen wall pockets go from an obscure item, for us, to a real popular collectable. Of course, their price has gone up as fast, if not faster, than their popularity.

We still find a lot of antique malls and flea markets where some of the staff do not know what a wall pocket is until we explain what they look like. And we never take anyone's word that there aren't any in the mall or shop. You would be surprised at how many we find after being told there aren't any. Of course, that's what makes collecting so much fun.

We don't claim to know everything there is to know about wall pockets. I don't think anyone can, for there are so many different ones. But we have done the best we can with displaying and pricing and sharing the information that we found to teach you what little we do know.

One very interesting thing is, women really used wall pockets for what they were intended for, which is rooting plants. They were sometimes called "rooters" and most of the ones we buy are very dirty inside. Even the most fragile ones have dirt or lime deposits in them. I've spent many hours washing mine. To me, clean is prettier.

We have also found planters identical to wall pockets except that they do not have the hole in back for hanging up. Most of the planters we have found were made by American potteries although I'm sure there are some from other countries.

Our main reason for writing this book is to help make people more aware of what wall pockets are. Of the few people we have talked to who collect wall pockets, most collect a specific kind: Roseville, Hull, Noritake, etc. But these are very expensive wall pockets and most of us can't afford them. Hopefully, this book will show that even the less expensive ones are beautiful and well worth collecting.

California Potteries

Most California pottery came from Southern California's pottery industry around the Los Angeles area. The multitude of large to small companies produced big to small lines of products. Documented history shows the span of production of wall pockets from the late twenties up into the sixties.

ROW 1:
1. Pink flower, mark, "#2 Block Pottery California." $15.00 - $20.00

2. Green flower, mark, paper label, "Genuine Porcelain, 22K Gold, Hand Decorated, Beachcomber's, California." $15.00 - $20.00

3. Yellow flower, mark, "Block Pottery, California #2." $15.00 - $20.00

ROW 2:
1. Yellow shell, mark, "California Art's." $15.00 - $20.00

2. Dust Pan, mark, "California." $10.00 - $15.00

3. Pink flower, mark, "Hibiscus California Art's." $20.00 - $25.00

ROW 3:
1. Leaves, mark, "721 - USA Calif. org.," also paper label, "California Originals Manhattan Beach, Calif." $25.00 - $30.00

2. Pink diaper, mark, "Cleminsons Seal c." $10.00 - $15.00

3. Leaves, mark, "721 - USA Calif. orig." No label. $25.00 - $30.00

                                             Price per pair - $55.00 - $75.00

ROW 4:
1. Coffee pot, mark, "Cleminsons Seal, Hand Painted c." $20.00 - $30.00

2. Kitchen scene, mark, "Cleminsons Seal, Hand Painted c." $20.00 - $30.00

3. Pitcher and bowl, mark "Cleminsons Seal, Hand Painted c." $20.00 - $30.00

All Cleminsons Pottery was made at El Monte, Calif. 1941 - 1963.

1

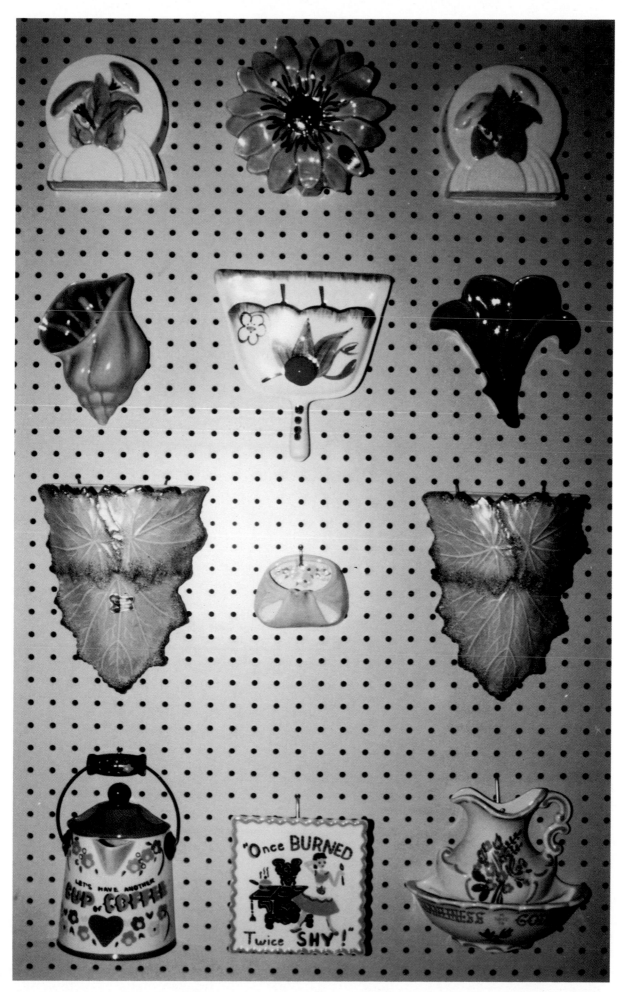

California Potteries

ROW 1:

    1.   Pear, mark, "Made in Calif. 303." $10.00 - $15.00

    2.   Rooster, mark, "Made in Calif. USA - CWP." $30.00 - $40.00

ROW 2:

    1.   Stove, mark, "Made in California." $10.00 - $15.00

    2.   Branch, mark, "Dadson Calif. 9." $30.00 - $35.00

    3.   Stove, mark, "Made in California." $10.00 - $15.00

ROW 3:

    1.   Skunk, mark, "8204," Identified as a DE LEE $20.00 - $35.00
        ART hand painted "skunkette," Los Angeles,
        Calif. Late forties.

    2.   Lamp, mark, "Don Jay Ceramics, Made in $15.00 - $25.00
        California."

    3.   Aqua Art, mark, "Don Rolen Hand Made $10.00 - $15.00
        #104 - of California."

ROW 4:

    1.   Rooster, mark, "Duran's - Royal Calif. '53." $20.00 - $30.00

    2.   Hen, mark, "Duran's - Royal Calif. '53." $25.00 - $35.00
                             Price per pair - $50.00 - $75.00

    3.   Fish, mark, "Gilner - Calif. C." $15.00 - $20.00

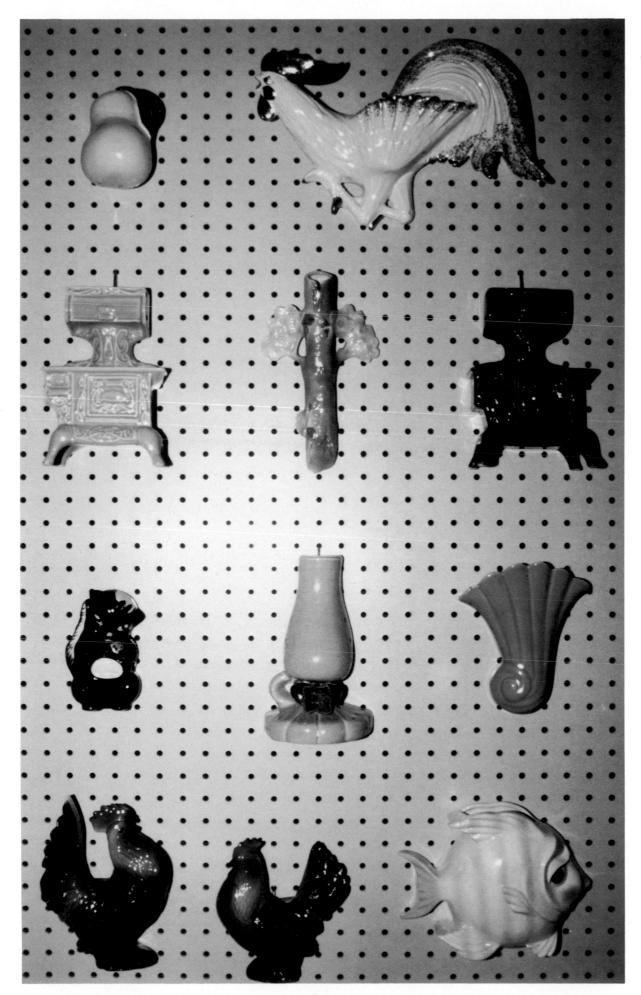

4

California Potteries

ROW 1:

1. Grapes, mark, "Gilner - Calif. C." $25.00 - $35.00

2. Deer, mark, "Gilner G - 550." $30.00 - $40.00

3. Fish, mark, "Gilner c." $25.00 - $35.00

   Gilner pottery was made at Culver City, California.

ROW 2:

1. Trivet, mark, "Hollywood Ceramics c Made in Calif." $20.00 - $30.00

2. Stove, no mark, Identified as Hollywood Ceramics. $25.00 - $35.00

3. Trivet, mark, "Hollywood Ceramics c Made in Calif." $20.00 - $30.00

ROW 3:

1. Chef on Stove, mark, "Hollywood Ceramics c." $25.00 - $35.00

2. Mammy by Washer, mark, "Hollywood Ceramics c Pat. Pend." $125.00 - $150.00

3. Chef on Stove, mark, "Hollywood Ceramics c." $25.00 - $35.00

ROW 4:

1. Skillet, mark, "Jans of California." $10.00 - $15.00

2. Broom, mark, "L & F Ceramics c Hollywood - Hand Made." $15.00 - $20.00

3. Hat, mark, "KTEK - Calif. Hand Made #43." $40.00 - $50.00
   Extra nice and heavy and looks like stoneware.

California Potteries

ROW 1:

1. Women, mark, "L & F Ceramics Made in California." $15.00 - $20.00

2. Man, mark, "L & F Ceramics Made in California." $15.00 - $20.00

    Price per pair- $35.00 - $45.00

3. Skillet, mark, "Hand Made - original Marcelle, Moran, California." $10.00 - $15.00

ROW 2:

1. Teapot, mark, "Maurice of California c USA -KWI." $15.00 - $25.00

2. Leaf, mark, "Poppytrail by Metlox." Metlox Potteries, 1927 - 1989 Manhattan Beach, Calif. Poppytrail became a line the first time in 1934 until 1942, came out again 1958, popular for a few years and back again in 1978. The paper labels on this wall pocket put it being made during the sixties and seventies. $30.00 - $40.00

3. Hat, mark, "Stewart G. McCullock c Calif." $10.00 - $15.00

ROW 3:

1. Elf by Well, mark, paper label "Treasure Craft, c South Gate, California." $15.00 - $25.00

2. Pear, mark, "Treasure Craft, c South Gate, California." $15.00 - $20.00

3. Elf on Leaf, no mark, Identified as Treasure Craft. $20.00 - $30.00

ROW 4:

1. Apple, no mark Identified as Treasure Craft. $15.00 - $20.00

2. Apple, mark, "Treasure Craft, California." $15.00 - $20.00

3. Apple, mark, "Treasure Craft, South Gate, California." Treasure Craft 1945 - 1988, South Gate, California, also known as Pottery Craft, Compton, California. In 1988 the company was purchased by Pfaltzgraff of York, Pennsylvania. $15.00 - $20.00

7

California Potteries

ROW 1:

1. Fish, mark, "Tropic Treasures By Ceramicraft, San Clemente, Calif. Pat. NO. D - 169, 159." $15.00 - $20.00

2. Pear, mark, "Hand Painted, Vernell, Calif." $15.00 - $20.00

ROW 2:

1. Left Leaf, mark, "West Coast Pottery 916 Calif." $15.00 - $20.00

2. Peacock, mark, "West Coast Pottery, California USA - 441." $35.00 - $50.00

3. Right Leaf, mark, "West Coast Pottery 916 Calif." $15.00 - $20.00
   Price per pair - $35.00 - $50.00

ROW 3:

1. Left Leaf, mark, "West Coast Pottery 916 Calif." $10.00 - $15.00

2. Right Leaf, mark, "West Coast Pottery 916 Calif." $10.00 - $15.00
   Price per pair - $25.00 - $35.00

West Coast Potteries, Burbank, California. Above pair have an original old store price tag marked $4.95 per pair.

ROW 4:

1. Blue with Bamboo, mark, "MW - 2106" $12.00 - $15.00

2. Blue with Bamboo, mark "MW - 2106 Hand Decorated Weil Ware, Picture of a Burro, made in California, DES. PAT. APPL. FOR. $12.00 - $15.00

10

Czechoslovakian

Czechoslovakia is very popular for all types of collectibles. History shows glassware and pottery was made as early as the thirteenth century, and is still being made today. Most of this glassware and pottery can be referred to as: unusual, especially nice, particularly elaborate, and beautifully crafted.

ROW 1:
1. Orange, mark, "Trade Mark, Crown, Coronet, Czechoslovakia Registered." $40.00 - $50.00

2. Orange and Silver, mark, "Made in Czechoslovakia." $70.00 - $85.00

3. Multi-color, mark, "Trade mark, Crown Coronet, Czechoslovakia Registered." $40.00 - $50.00

ROW 2:
1. Bird, mark, "Made in Czechoslovakia." $45.00 - $55.00

2. Purple and Yellow, mark, "Czechoslovakia 447." $45.00 - $55.00

3. Bird, mark, "Made in Czechoslovakia 5671 - B." $50.00 - $60.00

ROW 3:
1. Bird, mark, "Made in Czechoslovakia 5676 - A." $45.00 - $50.00

2. Parrot, mark, "Made in Czechoslovakia." $45.00 - $50.00

3. Bird, mark, "Made in Czechoslovakia 5860 - A." $50.00 - $55.00

ROW 4:
1. Bird, mark, "Made in Czechoslovakia 5675 - A." $45.00 - $50.00

2. Bird, mark, "Made in Czechoslovakia 5760 - A." $45.00 - $50.00

Frankoma

Frankoma Pottery was started by John Frank as the Frank Potteries in 1933. It is still in operation in Sapulpa, Oklahoma offering a full line of art pottery and dinnerware. The factory burned down twice, but was rebuilt. John Frank died in 1973 and his daughter, Joniece, has directed the business since his death.

ROW 1:

    1.   Acorn, green and brown, mark, "Frankoma 190." $15.00 - $25.00

    2.   Acorn, brown and green, mark, "Frankoma 190." $15.00 - $25.00

ROW 2:

    1.   Acorn, brown, mark, "190 Frankoma." $15.00 - $25.00

    2.   Leaves, brown, mark "Frankoma 197." $45.00 - $60.00

    3.   Acorn, brown, mark "190 Frankoma." $15.00 - $25.00

ROW 3:

    1.   Acorn, light brown, mark, "Frankoma 190." $15.00 - $25.00

    2.   Acorn, red, mark, "Frankoma 190." $15.00 - $25.00

    3.   Acorn, green, mark "Frankoma 190." $15.00 - $25.00

Frankoma

ROW 1:

1. Boot, left, brown and tan, mark, "Frankoma 133." $15.00 - $25.00

2. Boot, right, brown and tan, mark, "Frankoma 133." $15.00 - $25.00

3. Old original color.   Price per pair - $35.00 - $60.00

ROW 2:

1. Boot, right, grey speckled, mark, "Frankoma 133." $15.00 - $25.00

2. Boot, right, clay brown, mark, "Frankoma 133." $15.00 - $25.00

3. Boot, right, brown, mark, "Frankoma 133." $15.00 - $25.00

ROW 3:

1. Boot, right, green, mark, "Frankoma 133." $15.00 - $25.00

2. Boot, right, brown and tan, mark, "Frankoma 133." $15.00 - $25.00

3. Boot, right, black, mark, "Frankoma 133." $15.00 - $25.00

Frankoma

ROW 1:

1. Boot, left, mauve, mark, "Frankoma 133." $15.00 - $25.00

2. Boot, left, light blue, mark, "Frankoma 133." $15.00 - $25.00

3. Boot, left, rose, mark, "Frankoma 133." $15.00 - $25.00

ROW 2:

1. Boot, left, brown and green, mark, "Frankoma 133." $15.00 - $25.00

2. Boot, left, dark brown, mark, "Frankoma 133." $15.00 - $25.00

3. Boot, left, green and brown, mark, "Frankoma 133." $15.00 - $25.00

ROW 3:

1. Boot, left, tan, mark, "Frankoma 133." $15.00 - $25.00

2. Boot, left, dark brown, mark, "Frankoma 133." $15.00 - $25.00

3. Boot, left, brown and tan, mark, "Frankoma 133." $15.00 - $25.00

ROW 4:

Boot, left, dark blue mark, "Frankoma 133." $15.00 - $25.00

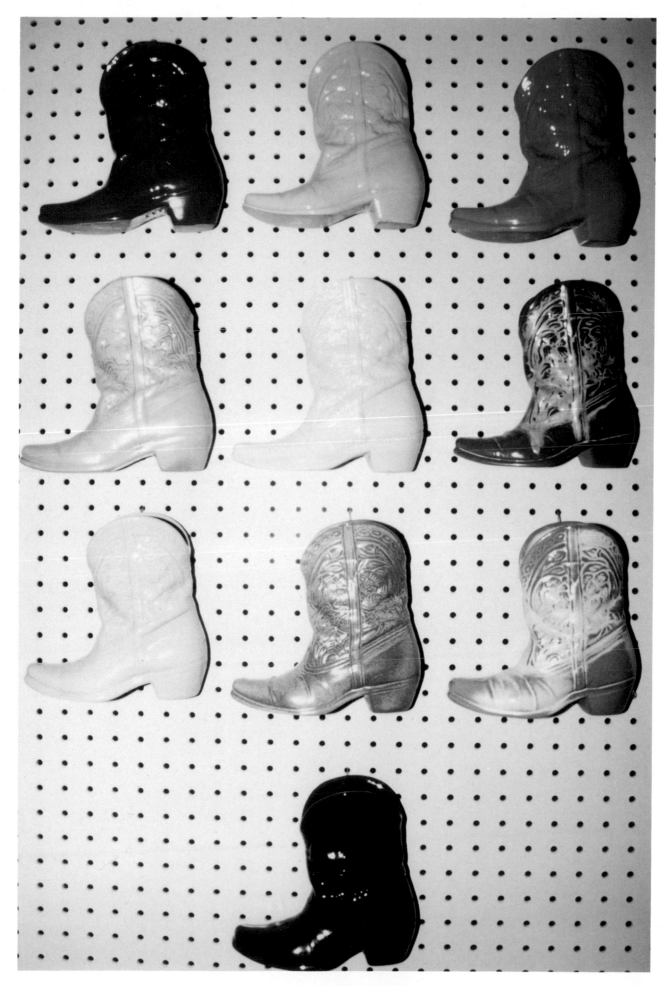

18

Germany

Finding a wall pocket marked "Germany" is like finding a treasure. We have hunted high and low and have found very few and have only five in our collection. They are hard to find and usually very expensive. Most are highly decorated on fine porcelain, and are of quality workmanship.

ROW 1:

1. Juggler, porcelain, hand painted, luster finish, $95.00 - $110.00
mark, "G-DEP-16071 Germany."

2. Joker, porcelain, hand painted, trimmed with $60.00 - $75.00
gold, mark, "Germany 16571-G-DEP."

ROW 2:

Parrot, mark, "Trade Mark-Coronet, Registered $50.00 - $65.00
Germany 10151-2."

ROW 3:

1. Angel, porcelain, hand painted, trimmed with gold, $55.00 - $75.00
mark, paper label "Germany."

2. Yellow Wizard, porcelain, hand painted, mark, $60.00 - $75.00
"Germany B-8795."

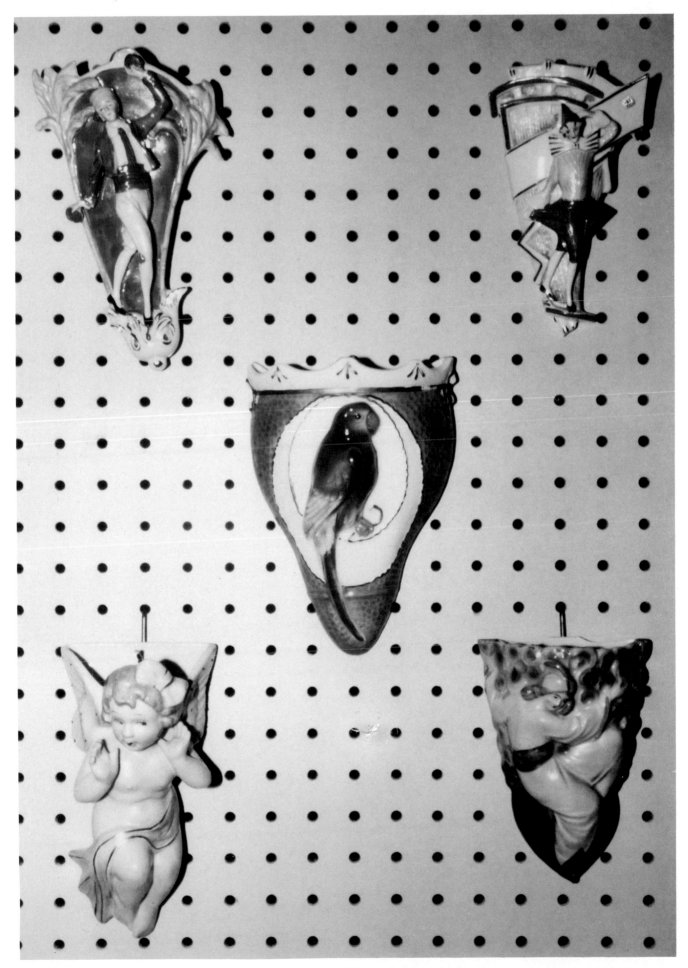

Glass

ROW 1:

1.   Black glass, Amethyst, appears black until held $40.00 - $55.00
to a bright light, then a dark purple can be seen.
It has been manufactured by many companies
from mid 1800's until today. No mark.

2.   Marigold Carnival glass, no mark. $40.00 - $55.00

ROW 2:

Bird with marigold Carnival glass, mark, paper $50.00 - $75.00
label "Patent Pending Syroco Wood, made in
USA, Syracuse, N.Y." Used only as a Rooter
with Water.

ROW 3:

1.   Woodpecker pattern, no mark, Marigold Carnival $85.00 - $110.00
glass. It has only been found in marigold color.
Made by Northwood Glass Company of Indiana,
Pennsylvania between 1908 to 1923.

2.   Bird and grapes, Marigold Carnival glass, no $85.00 - $110.00
mark. Made during the carnival glass era 1908
to 1923. This pattern has only been found on this
wall pocket.

Glass

ROW 1:
    1.   Clear depression type glass, Anniversary $30.00 - $40.00
            pattern. No mark. Made by Jeannette
            Glass Company 1947 - 1949.

    2.   Clear glass, no mark, grape pattern. $30.00 - $40.00

ROW 2:
    1.   Black matt finish with hand painted flowers $30.00 - $40.00
            applied on a clear depression type glass. No
            mark.

    2.   Green frosted finish trimmed with blue stripes, $30.00 - $40.00
            applied on a clear depression type glass. No
            mark.

ROW 3:

        Canoe, Vaseline glass with daisy and button $45.00 - $60.00
        pattern. Vaseline glass is a greenish-yellow
        color made by adding uranium oxide during
        the manufacturing of glass in the Victorian era
        or late 1800's. Vaseline glass is still being made
        today, but is being colored by a different process.

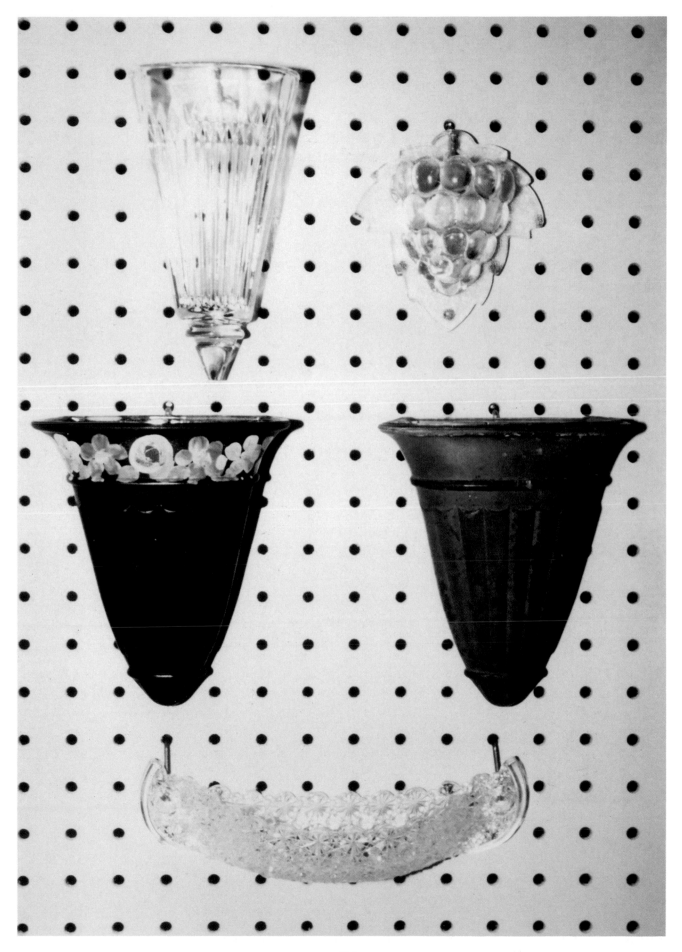

Haeger

Haeger Potteries Inc., originating in 1871, at the present has three plants in Illinois making vases, flower pots, novelty planters and some very nice wall pockets. They have a showroom in Dundee, Illinois, and have a very large number of visitors per year.

ROW 1:

1. Lady head, mark, green label, "HAEGER MADE IN USA." Original price tag on back, sold for $10.00 new. $25.00 - $30.00

2. Grapes, mark "ROYAL HAEGER R-745 USA." $15.00 - $25.00

ROW 2:

1. Green art, mark, green label, "HAEGER MADE IN USA." $15.00 - $25.00

2. Bird house, mark, "ROYAL HAEGER BY ROYAL HICKMAN, R-287-USA." $25.00 - $30.00

ROW 3:

1. Mauve leaves, mark, green and silver label, "GENUINE HAEGER POTTERY 75TH ANNIVERSARY." This was made in 1947. $30.00 - $40.00

2. Gray flower, mark, "ROYAL HAEGER R-1135-USA." $10.00 - $15.00

ROW 4:

1. Fish, green and white, mark, gold color crown shaped label, "ROYAL HAEGER©." $17.00 - $25.00

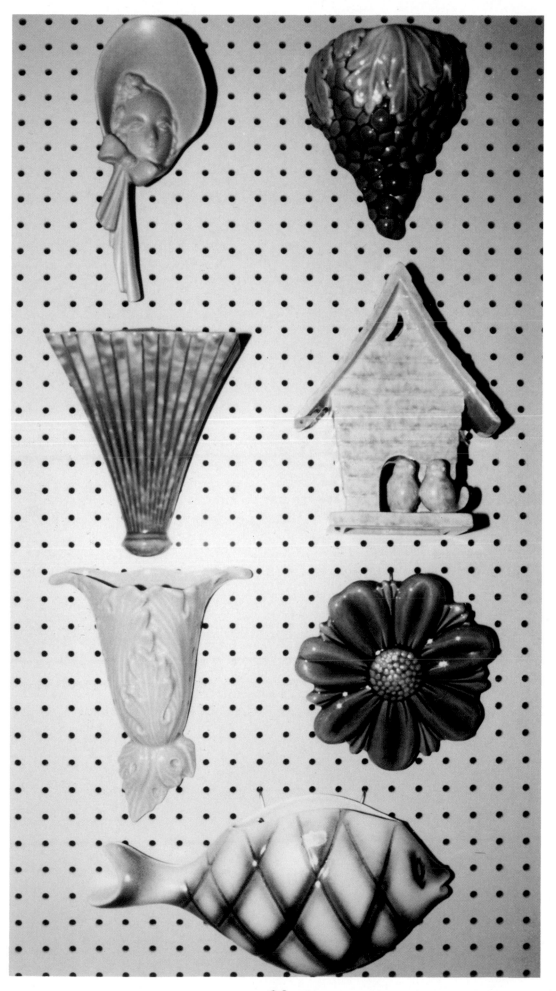

26

Haeger

ROW 1:

1. Floral gray design, mark, paper label, "GENUINE HAEGER." $10.00 - $15.00

2. Oriental lady, trimmed with gold, no mark. It is 12 inches tall. $30.00 - $40.00

3. Floral white design, no mark. $10.00 - $15.00

ROW 2:

1. Floral aqua color design, mark, paper label, "GENUINE HAEGER." $10.00 - $15.00

2. Oriental lady, trimmed with gold, no mark. It is 12 inches tall.   Price per pair - $30.00 - $40.00
$65.00 - $90.00

3. Floral aqua color design, mark, paper label, "GENUINE HAEGER."   Price per pair - $22.00 - $35.00

Hull

Hull Pottery Company, Crooksville, Ohio, operated from 1905 until 1986. Labor problems, the high cost of fuel and foreign competition forced Hull Pottery to close in March 1986, but for the 81 years they were in business, they made some of the most beautiful pottery in the country.

ROW 1:

1. Shell, Royal Woodland, pink and gray, mark, "W 13 7 1/2 HULL USA." Made in the 1950's. $50.00 - $75.00

2. Pitcher, Sunglow, yellow, mark, "USA 81." Made in 1952. $50.00 - $75.00

ROW 2:

1. Whisk broom, Sunglow, yellow, mark, "USA 82." Made in 1952. $50.00 - $75.00

2. Whisk broom, Sunglow, pink, mark, "USA 82." Made in 1952. $50.00 - $75.00

ROW 3:

1. Flying goose, blue and pink, mark, "Hull 67 USA." Made in 1950's. $45.00 - $60.00

2. Shell, Woodland gloss, pink, mark, "W 13 7 1/2 Hull USA." Made in 1950's. No hole for hanging. Indentation on front, but hole wasn't punched. $75.00 - $125.00

30

Hull

ROW 1:

1.   Iron, Sunglow, pink, no mark. Made in 1952. $55.00 - $90.00

2.   Leaves and berries, green, mark, "Hull 112 USA." Made in 1952. $40.00 - $50.00

3.   Pitcher, Bow-Knot, pink, mark, "B 26 6 USA Hull Art." Made in 1949. $140.00 - $200.00

ROW 2:

1.   Whisk broom, Bow-Knot, pink, mark, "B 27 8." Made in 1949. $140.00 - $200.00

2.   Whisk broom, Bow-Knot, blue, mark, "B 27 8." Made in 1949. $140.00 - $200.00

3.   Cup and saucer, Bow-Knot, blue, mark, "B 24 6." Made in 1949. $140.00 - $200.00

ROW 3:

1.   Cup and saucer, Sunglow, pink, mark, "80 6 1/4." Made in 1952. $55.00 - $90.00

2.   Little Red Riding Hood, by Hull and Regal. Made 1943 thru 1957. $400.00 - $700.00

3.   Shell, Woodland gloss, green, mark, "W 13 7 1/2." Made in the 1950's. $75.00 - $125.00

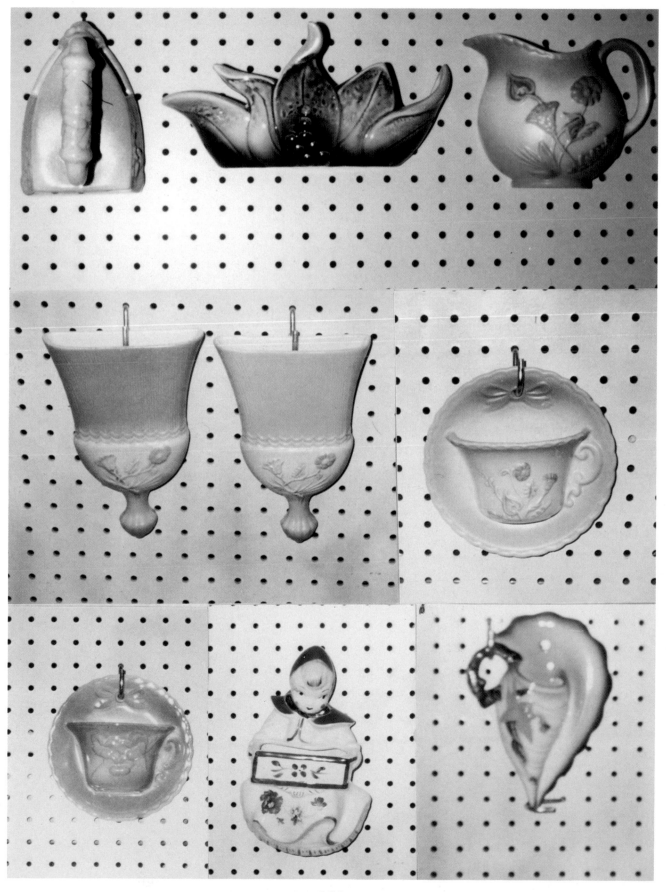

Hummel

Hummel made only three wall pockets, 360-A, 360-B and 360-C. We show only 360-A on the opposite page as we have been unable to find the other two. They are all made on the same design, except 360-B has the boy alone, and 360-C has the girl alone. They were introduced in the late 1950's and made into the 1960's, discontinued for a few years, then re-introduced in the 1970's. The earlier ones with the "Stylized Bee" mark are much higher priced than the later ones. These wall pockets did not sell as well as other Hummel pieces, possibly because wall pockets were not as popular in the 1950's and 1960's as they were in the 1930's and 1940's. They are very difficult to find.

ROW 1:

Boy and Girl, mark "PAINTED BY MT - 1983, $135.00 - $160.00
360-A GOEBEL W. GERMANY 1958."

The 1958 is incised into the back.

Japan
LUSTERWARE

This is the only chapter which will have a picture page made up of some unique wall pockets that include a beautiful hand carved, wood oriental picture, and some of the finest crafted Lusterware finished wall pockets. The wall pockets will be shown again and priced on the following pages.

Japanese Lusterware finish is a metallic type of coloring giving an iridescent metal-like look. Japanese craftsmen employed this technique in the manufacturing of wall pockets from the 1920's through 1941. The Lusterware was made and imported from Japan, mostly during the early twenties, but continued up until the start of World War II, in 1941.

When buying Lusterware make sure the finish is bright and shiny. Harsh soaps and hard rubbing can ruin the finish, as can the labels some dealers put on the front of a Lusterware wall pocket. Wash them with mild soap and warm water. Dry with a soft cloth. Please don't put sticky labels on them. A string label can be used.

PLEASE HELP TO PRESERVE THE LUSTERWARE FINISH

(Photos on page 36 are shown throughout this chapter.)

36

Japan Lusterware

ROW 1:

1. Red and white flowers, mark, in red letters, "HAND PAINTED (BIRD) MADE IN JAPAN." $30.00 - $45.00

2. White bird on limb, mark, in red letters, "MADE IN JAPAN." $55.00 - $75.00

3. Pink flowers, mark, in red letters, "HAND PAINTED (BIRD) MADE IN JAPAN." $30.00 - $45.00

ROW 2:

1. Blue and white flowers, mark, in red letters, "HAND PAINTED (H) JAPAN." $35.00 - $50.00

2. Parrot and pink flowers, mark, in red letters, "HAND PAINTED (H) JAPAN." $35.00 - $50.00

3. Yellow flower, mark, in black letters, "(SNAIL) MADE IN JAPAN." $35.00 - $50.00

ROW 3:

1. Peacock. Wall pocket color is gray top with yellow bottom, mark, in red letters, "HAND PAINTED (H) JAPAN." $40.00 - $55.00

2. Peacock. Wall pocket color is tan top with blue bottom, mark, in red letters, "HAND PAINTED (H) JAPAN." $40.00 - $55.00

3. Red and white flowers, mark, in red letters, "HAND PAINTED (H) JAPAN." $35.00 - $50.00

38

Japan Lusterware

ROW 1:

1. Sailing ship, mark, in black letters, "MADE IN JAPAN." $35.00 - $50.00

2. Tree, mark, in gold letters, "MADE IN JAPAN." $45.00 - $60.00

3. Bird and red flowers, mark, in red letters, "HAND PAINTED (H) JAPAN." $35.00 - $50.00

ROW 2:

1. Bird and white blossoms, mark, in red letters, "MADE IN JAPAN." $35.00 - $40.00

2. Woman's face, mark, in black letters, "MADE IN JAPAN." $60.00 - $80.00

3. Bird and white blossoms, mark, in red letters, "MADE IN JAPAN." Price per pair - $75.00 - $100.00

ROW 3:

1. White blossoms, mark, in red letters, "HAND PAINTED (H) JAPAN." $40.00 - $55.00

2. Blue flowers, mark, in black letters, "JAPAN-2." $35.00 - $50.00

3. White blossoms, mark, in red letters, "HAND PAINTED (H) JAPAN." Price per pair - $90.00 - $110.00

40

Japan Lusterware

ROW 1:

1. Bird on limb. Wall pocket color is blue top with tan bottom, mark, in red letters, "HAND PAINTED (H) JAPAN." $35.00 - $50.00

2. Bird on limb. Wall pocket color is tan top with mother of pearl bottom, mark, in red letters, "HAND PAINTED (H) JAPAN." $35.00 - $50.00

3. Bird on limb. Wall pocket color is blue top with tan bottom, mark, in red letters, "HAND PAINTED (H) JAPAN."   Price per pair - $75.00 - $105.00

ROW 2:

1. Red iris flower, mark, in red letters, "HAND PAINTED (H) JAPAN #2748." $35.00 - $50.00

2. Japanese house, mark, in red letters, "GOLD CASTLE (PAGODA) HAND PAINTED CHIKUSA MADE IN JAPAN." $50.00 - $65.00

3. Cherries, mark in red letters, "HAND PAINTED (H) JAPAN #2748." $35.00 - $50.00

ROW 3:

1. Yellow and red flowers. Orange color on bottom is plain. $35.00 - $50.00

2. Yellow and red flowers. Orange color on bottom is medium splashed. $35.00 - $50.00

3. Yellow and red flowers. Orange color on bottom is heavy splashed. All of the above three are marked the same in black letters, "HAND PAINTED (SNAIL) MADE IN JAPAN."   Price per pair - $75.00 - $105.00

42

Japan Lusterware

ROW 1:

1. Pink buds, mark, in red letters, "HAND PAINTED (BIRD) MADE IN JAPAN." $20.00 - $30.00

2. Boy playing violin, mark, in black letters, "JAPAN." $20.00 - $30.00

3. Yellow and blue flowers, mark, in red letters, "HAND PAINTED (BIRD) MADE IN JAPAN." $20.00 - $30.00

   Above #1 and #3 in the small size are hard to find and should bring premium price.

ROW 2:

1. Bird and flowers, mark, in red letters, "HAND PAINTED (H) JAPAN." $30.00 - $45.00

2. Flowers, mark, in red letters, "MADE IN JAPAN." $45.00 - $60.00

3. Flowers and basket, mark, in red letters, "HAND PAINTED (H) JAPAN #2748." $30.00 - $45.00

ROW 3:

1. Flying ducks, mark, in red letters, "HAND PAINTED (H) JAPAN." $40.00 - $55.00

2. Flying ducks, mark, in red letters, "HAND PAINTED (H) JAPAN." Same as above, but the colors are different. $40.00 - $55.00

3. Flying ducks, mark, in red letters, "HAND PAINTED (H) JAPAN."   Price per pair - $85.00 - $115.00

Japan Lusterware

ROW 1:

1. White goose, mark, in black letters, "MADE IN JAPAN." $20.00 - $30.00

2. Green bird, mark, in red letters, "HAND PAINTED (FLOWER) MADE IN JAPAN." $20.00 - $30.00

3. Blue and red bird, mark, in red letters, "HAND PAINTED (H) JAPAN." $20.00 - $30.00

ROW 2:

1. Blue and red bird, mark, in red letters, "HAND PAINTED (H) JAPAN." $35.00 - $50.00

2. Green bird, mark, in green letters, "HAND PAINTED (FLOWER) MADE IN JAPAN." $30.00 - $45.00

3. Mauve flower, mark in black letters, "MADE IN JAPAN." $30.00 - $45.00

ROW 3:

1. Flying bird, mark, in red letters, "HAND PAINTED (H) JAPAN." $35.00 - $50.00

2. Gray dragon, mark, in red letters, "HAND PAINTED (H) JAPAN." $35.00 - $50.00

3. Flying bird, mark, in red letters, "HAND PAINTED (H) JAPAN."   Price per pair - $75.00 - $105.00

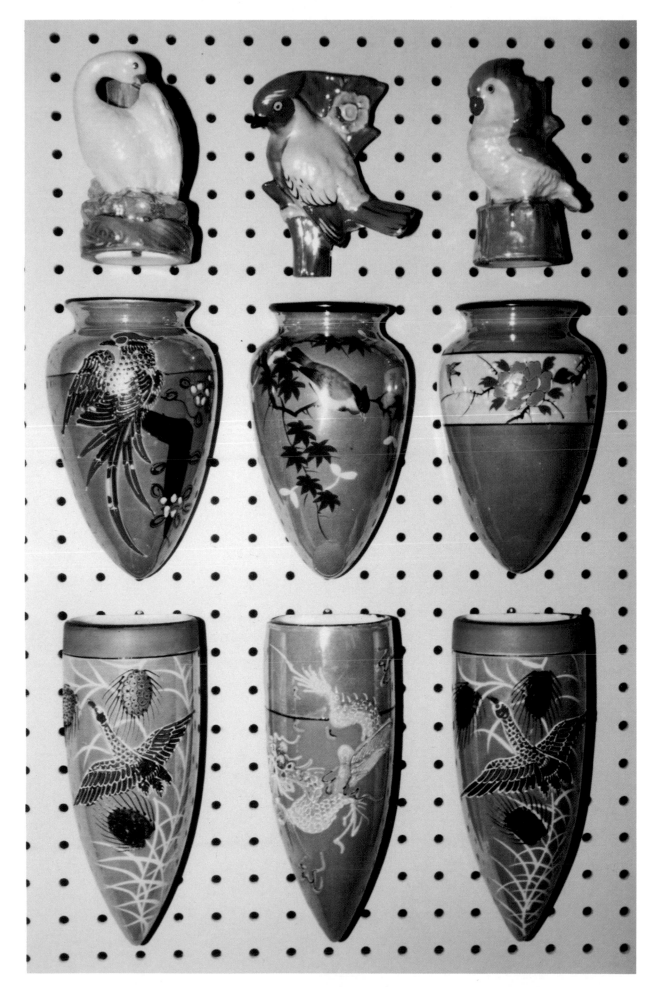

46

Japan Lusterware

ROW 1:

1. Bird and pink flowers, mark, in red letters, "MADE IN JAPAN." $20.00 - $30.00

2. Blue and yellow flowers, mark, in black letters, "HAND PAINTED TRICO NAGOYA JAPAN." $30.00 - $45.00

3. Yellow bird and pink flowers, mark, in red letters, "MADE IN JAPAN." $20.00 - $30.00

ROW 2:

1. Bird on limb, mark, in red letters, "HAND PAINTED (*) MADE IN JAPAN." $30.00 - $45.00

2. Tree, mark, in black letters, "MADE IN JAPAN." $35.00 - $50.00

3. Flying bird, mark, in black letters, "MADE IN JAPAN." $30.00 - $45.00

ROW 3:

1. 1, 2, and 3 are all the same color and pattern, but note how the lowest flower is in a different place on the lines. They are all marked in black letters, "GOLD CASTLE (PAGODA) HAND PAINTED CHIKUSA MADE IN JAPAN."

   Price each - $30.00 - $45.00
   Price per pair - $65.00 - $95.00

48

Japan
Noritake

Japan started producing NORITAKE in 1904. It is best known for china dinnerware but also made some very beautiful wall pockets. The M in the backstamp on these wall pockets stands for the Morimuri Brothers who were the forerunners in the foreign trade for Japan. This backstamp was used as early as 1918 until 1941.

ROW 1:
1. Multi-flowers on red, mark, in red letters, "NORITAKE (M) HAND PAINTED MADE IN JAPAN." $80.00 - $105.00

ROW 2:
1. Red roses on tan lusterware, mark, in green letters, "NORITAKE (M) HAND PAINTED MADE IN JAPAN." $85.00 - $110.00

2. Red roses on tan lusterware, mark, in green letters, "NORITAKE (M) HAND PAINTED MADE IN JAPAN." $85.00 - $110.00

ROW 3:
1. House and tree on blue lusterware, mark, in red letters, "NORITAKE (M) HAND PAINTED MADE IN JAPAN." $85.00 - $110.00

Japan
Occupied

Items marked "Occupied Japan" were made during the years that the United States occupied Japan (1945 to 1952). Any item that was exported to the United States was supposed to be marked "Occupied Japan", but many were not. We find identical pieces marked "Japan" or "Made in Japan". The ones with the "Occupied Japan" mark are the most collectible and have a good value because of the scarcity of the pieces.

ROW 1:

1. Oriental dancer, mark, in green letters, "MADE IN OCCUPIED (M-R) JAPAN." $20.00 - $30.00

ROW 2:

1. Lady, blond hair, mark, in red letters, "MADE IN OCCUPIED JAPAN." $12.50 - $15.00

2. Man, mark, in red letters, "MADE IN OCCUPIED JAPAN." Original price on back - 29 cents. $12.50 - $15.00

3. Lady, brown hair, mark, in red letters, "MADE IN OCCUPIED JAPAN." Original price on back 29 cents. $12.50 - $15.00

    Above #2 and #3, price per pair - $25.00 - $35.00

ROW 3:

1. Japanese scene, mark, in red letters, "HAND PAINTED (FAN) IN OCCUPIED JAPAN." $25.00 - $35.00

Japan
Miscellaneous

The wall pockets on the next seven pages are what we have, until recently, called "THE OLD BLACK JAPAN", even though some of it is painted other colors. We could never find anyone that could tell us anything about it. We asked people who we felt were "experts," to no avail, until a short time ago. We stopped at an antique mall and there, sitting on a shelf in a booth, was a vase clipping from an old newspaper answering our questions. The finish on these wall pockets, made during the thirties, is supposed to simulate tree bark cloisonne (cloisonne over porcelain).

ROW 1:
1. Red and gold pagoda, mark, incised, "MADE IN JAPAN." $10.00 - $15.00

2. Red and gold pagoda, mark, incised, "MADE IN JAPAN." No red color on top rim. $10.00 - $15.00

3. Red and gold pagoda, mark, incised, "MADE IN JAPAN."   Price per pair - $22.00 - $32.00

ROW 2:
1. Red and yellow flowers, mark, incised, "MADE IN JAPAN." $15.00 - $20.00

2. Red bird and cherries, mark, incised, "MADE IN JAPAN." $40.00 - $50.00

3. Red and yellow flowers, mark, incised, "MADE IN JAPAN."   Price per pair - $32.00 - $42.00

ROW 3:
1. Red flowers, 6" long, mark, incised, "MADE IN JAPAN." $10.00 - $12.50

2. Red flowers, 6 3/4" long, mark, incised, "MADE IN JAPAN+." $12.50 - $15.00

3. Red flowers, 6" long, mark, incised, "MADE IN JAPAN."   Price per pair - $22.00 - $27.00

Japan Miscellaneous

ROW 1:

1. Red butterfly and trim, mark, incised, "MADE IN JAPAN." $15.00 - $20.00

2. Yellow and green flowers, mark, incised, "MADE IN JAPAN." $15.00 - $20.00

3. Red flower, mark, incised, "MADE IN JAPAN." $15.00 - $20.00

ROW 2:

1. Fancy design, mark, incised, "MADE IN JAPAN." $15.00 - $20.00

2. Red flowers, mark, incised, "MADE IN JAPAN." $25.00 - $35.00

3. Fancy design, mark, incised, "MADE IN JAPAN."
   Price per pair - $32.00 - $42.00

ROW 3:

1. Bird on limb, mark, incised, "MADE IN JAPAN." $12.50 - $17.50

2. Red and yellow flowers, mark, incised, "JAPAN (B) MADE IN JAPAN." $12.50 - $17.50

3. Red camel and green palm tree, mark, incised, "MADE IN JAPAN." $15.00 - $20.00

56

Japan Miscellaneous

ROW 1:
1. Copper color flowers, mark, incised, "MADE IN JAPAN." $10.00 - $15.00

2. Red flowers, mark, incised, "MADE IN JAPAN." $12.50 - $17.50

3. Copper color flowers, mark, incised, "MADE IN JAPAN."   Price per pair - $25.00 - $35.00

ROW 2:
1. Red, yellow and blue flowers, mark, incised, "MADE IN JAPAN." $10.00 - $15.00

2. Red flowers, mark, incised, "MADE IN JAPAN." $20.00 - $30.00

3. Red, yellow, and blue flowers, mark, incised, "MADE IN JAPAN."   Price per pair - $22.50 - $32.50

ROW 3:
1. Red, yellow and green flowers, mark, incised, "MADE IN JAPAN." $10.00 - $15.00

2. Pair of blue birds, mark, incised, "MADE IN JAPAN." $12.50 - $17.50

3. Red, yellow and green flowers, mark, incised, "MADE IN JAPAN."   Price per pair - $22.50 - $32.50

58

Japan Miscellaneous

ROW 1:

1. Copper color pagoda, plain top rim, mark, incised, "MADE IN JAPAN." $12.50 - $17.50

2. Blue flowers, mark, incised, "MADE IN JAPAN." $15.00 - $20.00

3. Copper color pagoda, fancy top rim, mark, incised "MADE IN JAPAN." $12.50 - $17.50

ROW 2:

1. Red flowers and berries, mark, incised, "MADE IN JAPAN." $12.50 - $17.50

2. Same as #1 and #3, but has better paint. $15.00 - $20.00

3. Red flowers and berries, mark, incised, "MADE IN JAPAN."   Price per pair - $30.00 - $40.00

ROW 3:

1. Silver color with red pagoda, mark, incised, "MADE IN JAPAN." $12.50 - $17.50

2. Cream color with red flowers, mark, incised, "MADE IN JAPAN." $15.00 - $20.00

3. Pink flower, mark, incised, "MADE IN JAPAN." $15.00 - $20.00

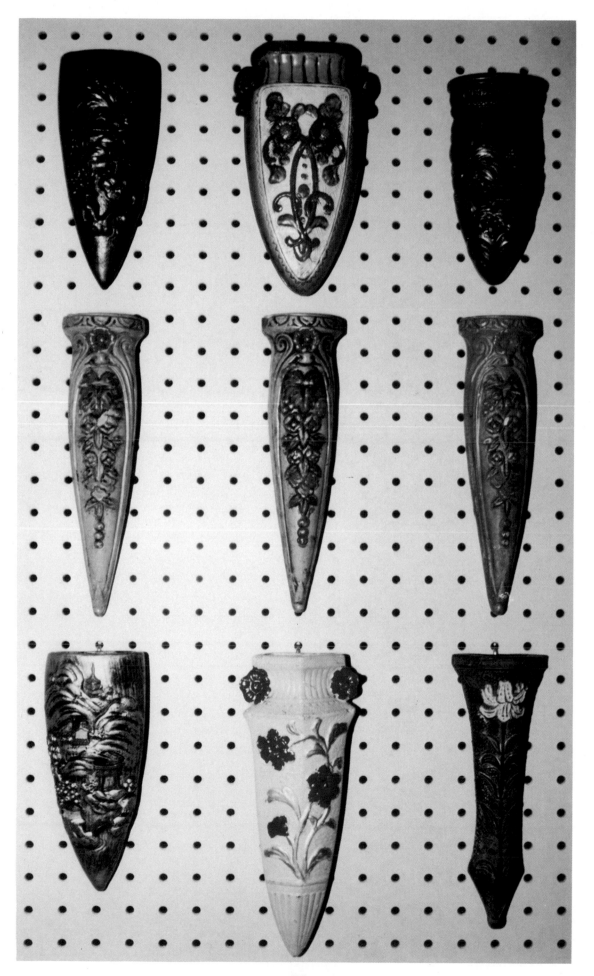

60

Japan Miscellaneous

ROW 1:

1. Blue and yellow, mark, incised, double marked, "MADE IN JAPAN - MADE IN JAPAN." $15.00 - $20.00

2. Fancy blue, yellow, green and red, mark, incised, "MADE IN JAPAN-Y." $15.00 - $20.00

3. Blue and yellow, mark, incised, double marked, "MADE IN JAPAN - MADE IN JAPAN."
   Price per pair - $35.00 - $45.00

ROW 2:

1. Red with yellow flowers, mark, incised, "MADE IN JAPAN-VT." $17.50 - $22.50

2. Big beautiful with red lacquer finish, birds on limbs, mark, incised, "MADE IN JAPAN." $45.00 - $60.00

3. Red with yellow flowers, mark, incised, "MADE IN JAPAN-VT."   Price per pair - $37.50 - $45.00

ROW 3:

1. Copper dragon, mark, incised, "MADE IN JAPAN." $10.00 - $15.00

2. Bronze color with red pagodas, mark, incised, "MADE IN JAPAN." $12.50 - $17.50

3. Copper dragon, mark, incised, "MADE IN JAPAN."   Price per pair - $22.50 - $32.50

Japan Miscellaneous

ROW 1:

1. Leaves and berries, mark, incised, "MADE IN JAPAN." $12.50 - $17.50

2. Gold color with flowers, mark incised, "MADE IN JAPAN." $12.50 - $17.50

3. Leaves and berries, mark, incised, "MADE IN JAPAN." Has fancy top rim and a small butterfly, mark, incised, "MADE IN JAPAN." $15.00 - $20.00

ROW 2:

1. Red flowers, mark, incised, "MADE IN JAPAN." $15.00 - $20.00

2. Pink flower, mark, incised, "HAND WARE HAND PAINTED MADE N JAPAN." $20.00 - $30.00

3. Red flowers, mark, incised, "MADE IN JAPAN."
Price per pair - $35.00 - $45.00

ROW 3:

1. Red with flowers, mark, incised, "MADE IN JAPAN-U." $20.00 - $25.00

2. Blue with flowers, mark, incised, "MADE IN JAPAN-U." $20.00 - $25.00

3. Red with flowers, mark, incised, "MADE IN JAPAN-U." Price per pair - $45.00 - $55.00

Japan Miscellaneous

ROW 1:

1. Red with dragon, mark, incised, "MADE IN JAPAN." $15.00 - $20.00

2. Fancy with red flower, mark, incised, "MADE IN JAPAN." $15.00 - $20.00

3. Red with dragon, mark, incised, "MADE IN JAPAN."   Price per pair - $35.00 - $45.00

ROW 2:

1. Green with flowers, mark, incised, "HAND MADE HAND PAINTED MADE IN JAPAN." $15.00 - $20.00

2. Hunter on horse with hunting dogs, mark, incised, "MADE IN JAPAN-U." $20.00 - $25.00

3. Copper color with orange flowers, mark, incised, "MADE IN JAPAN." $20.00 - $25.00

ROW 3:

1. Yellow with red bird, mark, incised, "MADE IN JAPAN." $12.50 - $17.50

2. Yellow with red dragon, mark, incised, "MADE IN JAPAN." $15.00 - $20.00

3. Green with faded flowers, mark, incised, "MADE IN JAPAN." $10.00 - $15.00

Japan Miscellaneous

ROW 1:

1. Goose with small handles, mark, in black letters, "MADE IN JAPAN." $20.00 - $25.00

2. Pitcher with green handle, mark, in black letters, "MADE IN JAPAN." $20.00 - $25.00

3. Goose with large handles, mark, in black letters, "MADE IN JAPAN." $20.00 - $25.00

ROW 2:

1. Green and brown, pointed bottom, mark, in black letters, "MADE IN JAPAN." $15.00 - $20.00

2. Yellow and orange swan, mark, in green letters, "MADE IN JAPAN." $20.00 - $25.00

3. Green and brown, flat bottom, mark, in black letters, "MADE IN JAPAN." $15.00 - $20.00

ROW 3:

1. Yellow with green leaf, mark, in green letters, "MADE IN JAPAN." $15.00 - $20.00

2. Bird and flowers, mark, in black letters, "MADE IN JAPAN." $20.00 - $25.00

3. Yellow with green oriental design, mark, in green letters, "MADE IN JAPAN." $15.00 - $20.00

Japan Miscellaneous

ROW 1:

1. Flowers, mark, incised, "MADE IN JAPAN." $10.00 - $15.00

2. Dragon, mark, in black letters, "MADE IN JAPAN." $15.00 - $20.00

3. Flowers, mark, incised, "MADE IN JAPAN."
   Price per pair - $22.50 - $30.00

ROW 2:

1. Yellow flower, mark, in black letters, "MADE IN JAPAN." $20.00 - $30.00

2. Blue flower, mark, in black letters, "MADE IN JAPAN." $15.00 - $25.00

3. Mauve flower, mark, in black letters, "MADE IN JAPAN." $20.00 - $30.00

ROW 3:

1. Brown urn, mark, in black letters, "MADE IN JAPAN." $15.00 - $20.00

2. Yellow and green urn, mark, in green letters, "MADE IN JAPAN." $15.00 - $20.00

3. Yellow and green, mark, in green letters, "MADE IN JAPAN." $15.00 - $20.00

Japan Miscellaneous

ROW 1:

    1.   Multi-color flowers, mark, in black letters, "MADE IN JAPAN." $20.00 - $25.00

    2.   Blue and yellow, mark, in black letters, MADE IN JAPAN." $20.00 - $25.00

    3.   Orange basket weave with plums, mark, incised, "MADE IN JAPAN." $20.00 - $25.00

ROW 2:

    1.   Blue bird on limb, mark, incised, "MADE IN JAPAN-V." $40.00 - $50.00

    2.   Yellow flowers, mark, in black letters, "MADE IN JAPAN." $20.00 - $30.00

    3.   Red bird and grapes, mark, incised, "MADE IN JAPAN-V." $30.00 - $35.00

ROW 3:

    1.   Multi-color flowers, mark, incised, "MADE IN JAPAN." $25.00 - $30.00

    2.   White geese, mark, incised, "MADE IN JAPAN." $20.00 - $30.00

    3.   Bird on limb, mark, incised, "MADE IN JAPAN." $30.00 - $35.00

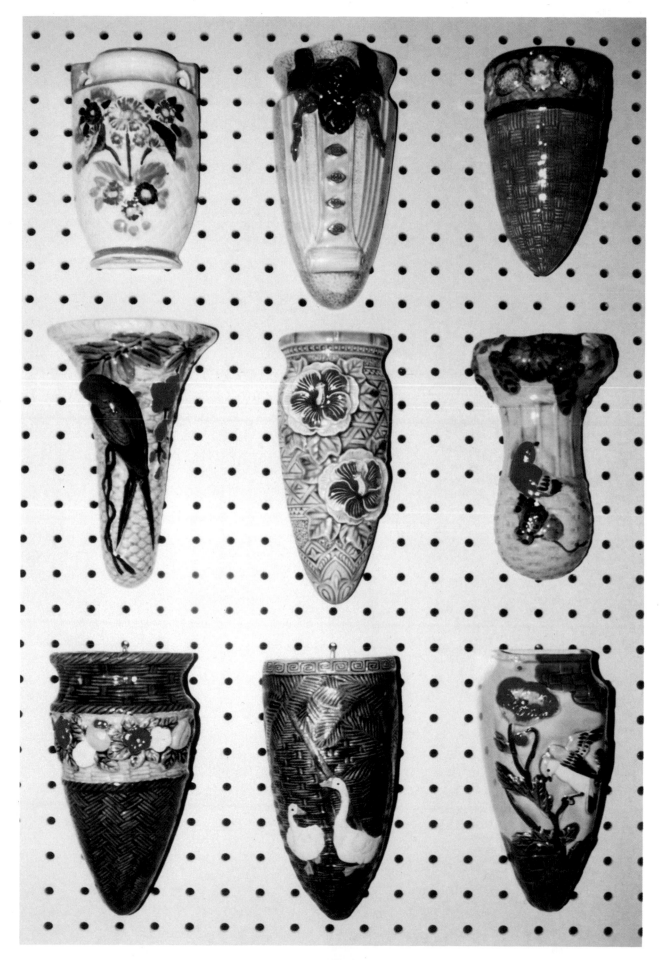

72

Japan Miscellaneous

ROW 1:

1. Woman in blue, mark, in black letters, "MADE IN JAPAN-MADE IN JAPAN," double marked. $15.00 - $20.00

2. Multi-color flowers, mark, incised, "MADE IN JAPAN." $15.00 - $20.00

3. Woman in blue, mark, in black letters, "MADE IN JAPAN-MADE IN JAPAN," double marked.

                             Price per pair - $35.00 - $45.00

ROW 2:

1. Dark green with yellow and orange flowers, has inner vase with cut-outs in outer shell, mark, incised, "MADE IN JAPAN." $50.00 - $65.00

2. Light green with flowers, mark, in black letters, "DAR CO., TROY, N.Y. -MADE IN JAPAN." $15.00 - $25.00

3. Dark green with yellow and orange flowers, has inner vase with cut-outs in outer shell, mark, incised, "MADE IN JAPAN."

                             Price per pair - $110.00 - $130.00

ROW 3:

1. White geese, mark, in black letters, "MADE IN JAPAN." $15.00 - $20.00

2. Bird on limb, mark, in black letters, "MADE IN JAPAN." $15.00 - $20.00

3. Yellow geese, mark, incised, "ANKOWARE MADE IN JAPAN-M." Same pattern as #1, but marked differently. $15.00 - $20.00

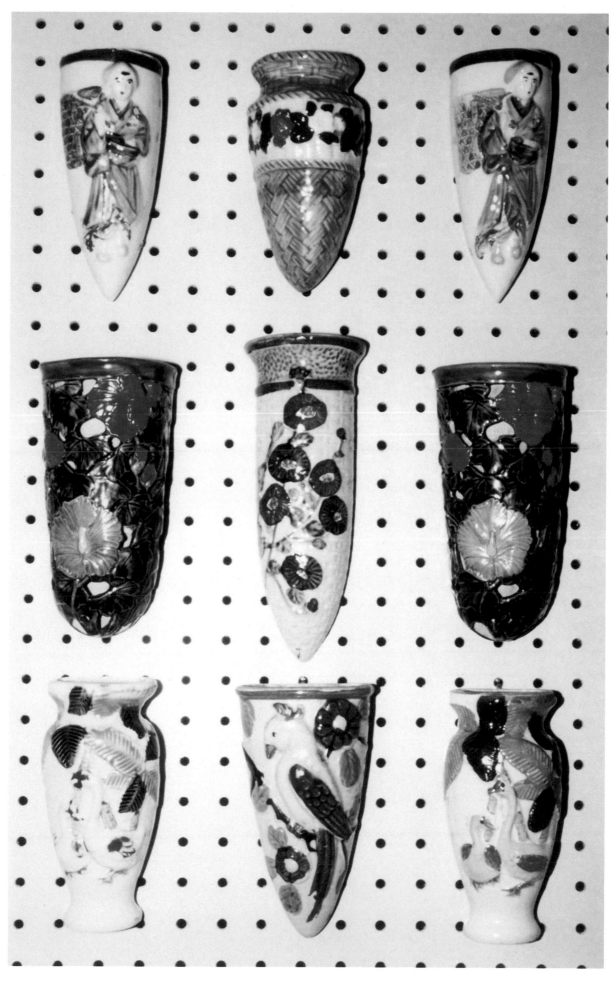

74

Japan Miscellaneous

ROW 1:

    1. Bird and mauve flowers, mark, in black letters, "MADE IN JAPAN." $20.00 - $25.00

    2. Bird and yellow flowers, mark, incised, "MADE IN JAPAN." $20.00 - $25.00

    3. Bird on limb, brown trim on top rim, mark, incised "MADE IN JAPAN." $15.00 - $20.00

ROW 2:

    1. Bird on limb with long mauve tail, mark, in black letters, "MADE IN JAPAN." $15.00 - $20.00

    2. Bird on limb on mauve color, mark, incised, "MADE IN JAPAN." $20.00 - $25.00

    3. Bird on limb with green tail, mark, incised, "MADE IN JAPAN." $10.00 - $15.00

ROW 3:

    1. Bird on limb, mark, in black letters, "MADE IN JAPAN." $10.00 - $15.00

    2. Bird and flowers, mark, in black letters, "MADE IN JAPAN." $10.00 - $15.00

    3. Bird on limb, mark, in black letters, "MADE IN JAPAN."   Price per pair - $25.00 - $35.00

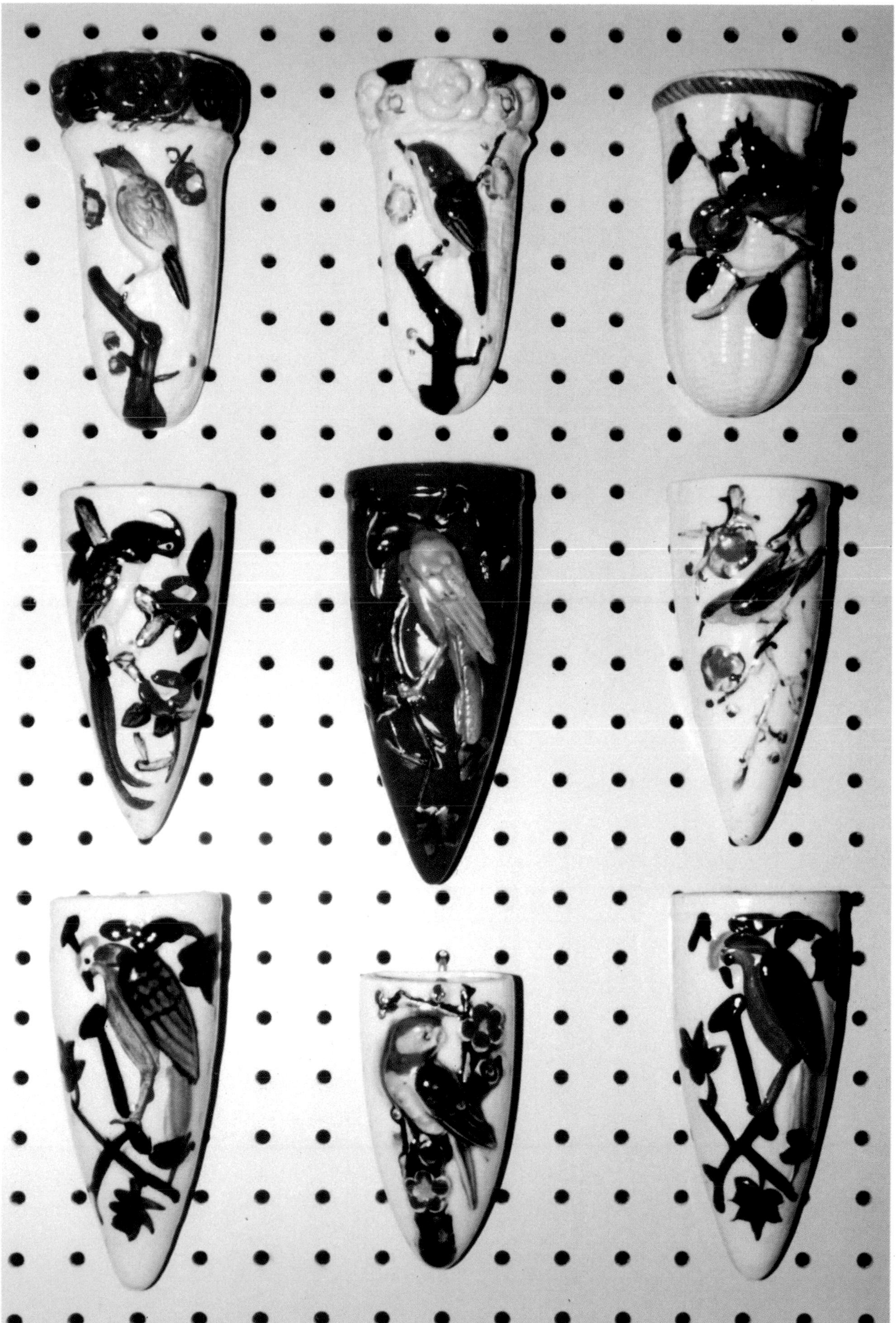

Japan Miscellaneous

ROW 1:

1. Green and yellow, mark, incised, "MADE IN JAPAN." $10.00 - $15.00

2. Blue and mauve flowers, mark, in black letters, "MADE IN JAPAN." $12.50 - $17.50

3. Green and yellow, mark, incised, "MADE IN JAPAN." Price per pair - $22.50 - $32.50

ROW 2:

1. Multi-color design, mark, incised, "MADE IN JAPAN." $15.00 - $20.00

2. Japanese woman trimmed with gold, mark, in red letters, "HAND PAINTED JAPAN (H) #2748." $25.00 - $40.00

3. Multi-color design, mark, incised, "MADE IN JAPAN." Price per pair - $35.00 - $45.00

ROW 3:

1. One mauve flower, mark incised, "MADE IN JAPAN." $10.00 - $15.00

2. Multi-color flowers, mark, incised, "MADE IN JAPAN-V." $25.00 - $30.00

3. Two multi-color flowers, mark, incised, "MADE IN JAPAN." $10.00 - $15.00

Japan Miscellaneous

ROW 1:

1. Boy, mark, double marked, in black letters, "MADE IN JAPAN, " and incised, "MADE IN JAPAN." $20.00 - $25.00

2. Dancing lady in black, mark, in red letters, "MADE IN JAPAN HAND PAINTED." $25.00 - $30.00

3. Boy, mark, double marked, in black letters, "MADE IN JAPAN, " and incised, "MADE IN JAPAN." Has brown tip on bottom.
Price per pair - $42.00 - $52.00

ROW 2:

1. Boy and basket, mark, in black letters, "MADE IN JAPAN." $20.00 - $25.00

2. Gray bird on limb, mark, in red letters, "HAND PAINTED (H) JAPAN." $35.00 - $45.00

3. Boy and basket, mark, in black letters, "MADE IN JAPAN."   Price per pair - $42.00 - $52.00

ROW 3:

1. Boy and basket, mark, in black letters, "MADE IN JAPAN." $20.00 - $25.00

2. Red bird on yellow, mark, in black letters, "MADE IN JAPAN." $15.00 - $20.00

3. Boy and basket, mark, in black letters, "MADE IN JAPAN."   Price per pair - $42.00 - $52.00

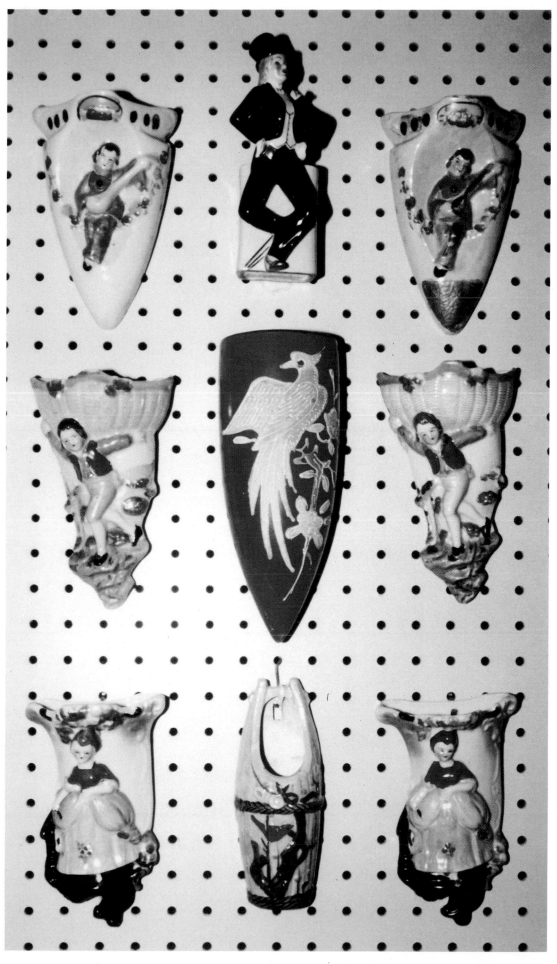

Japan Miscellaneous

ROW 1:

1. Boy and girl, 5 1/2" tall, mark, in red letters, "MADE IN JAPAN-Y." $20.00 - $25.00

2. Red and yellow roses trimmed in gold, mark, paper label, "NORLEANS JAPAN." $20.00 - $30.00

3. Boy and girl, 6 1/12" tall, mark, in red letters, "MADE IN JAPAN-Y," and incised, "MADE IN JAPAN." $20.00 - $25.00

ROW 2:

1. Girl and bird, mark, in red letters, "MADE IN JAPAN." $15.00 - $20.00

2. Bird and flowers, mark, in red letters, "GOLD CASTLE (PAGODA) HAND PAINTED CHIKUSA MADE IN JAPAN." $35.00 - $40.00

3. Boy, mark, in red letters, "MADE IN JAPAN." $15.00 - $20.00

       Above #1 and #3 price per pair - $35.00 - $45.00

ROW 3:

1. Man, mark, in black letters, "MADE IN JAPAN," and incised, "MADE IN JAPAN." $20.00 - $30.00

2. Lady on black, mark, incised, "MADE IN JAPAN." Wall pocket made of wood. $20.00 - $30.00

3. Lady, mark, in red letters, "JAPAN." $25.00 - $30.00

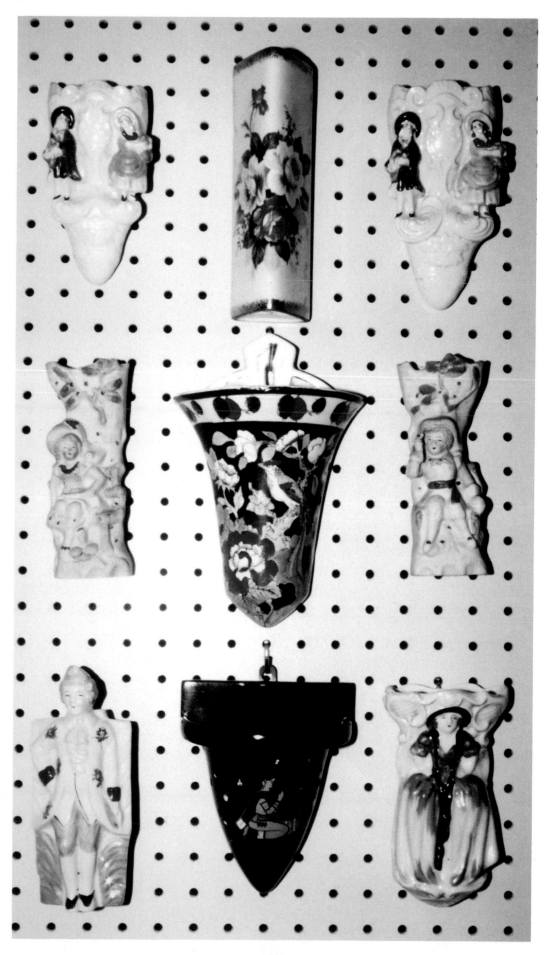

Japan Miscellaneous

ROW 1:

1.   Boy, mark, in black letters, "JAPAN." $15.00 - $20.00

2.   Pink flower trimmed with silver, mark, $10.00 - $15.00
in red letters, "MADE IN JAPAN."

3.   Deer head, mark, in black letters, "JAPAN." $12.50 - $15.00

ROW 2:

1.   Multi-color flowers trimmed with gold, mark, $10.00 - $15.00
incised, "MADE IN JAPAN-W 90."

2.   Roses with gold handles, mark, in red letters, $15.00 - $20.00
"MADE IN JAPAN."

3.   Multi-color flowers trimmed with gold, mark,
incised, "MADE IN JAPAN-W 90."
               Price per pair - $22.00 - $32.00

ROW 3:

1.   Cherub on green, mark, in blue letters, "JAPAN." $20.00 - $25.00

2.   Cherub on pink, mark, in black letters, "JAPAN." $20.00 - $25.00

3.   Cherub on green, mark, in blue letters, "JAPAN." $20.00 - $25.00
(Same as #1 but facing the opposite way.)

          Above #1 and #3 price per pair - $45.00 - $55.00

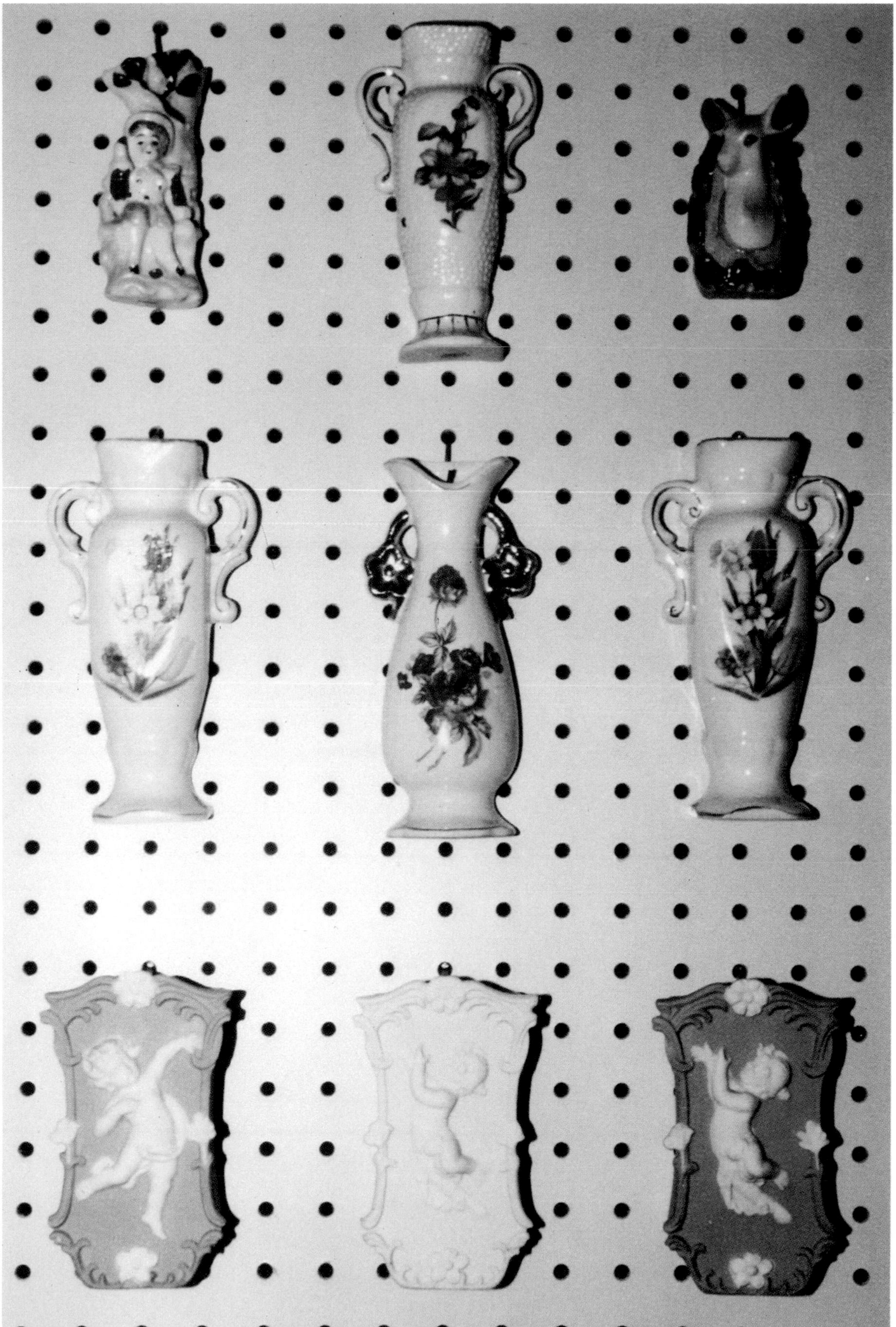

Japan Miscellaneous

ROW 1:

1. Baby and bird trimmed with silver, mark, in red letters, "JAPAN." $10.00 - $12.50

2. Pink rose, mark, paper label, "RICHARD JAPAN." $10.00 - $12.50

3. Baby trimmed with silver, mark, in red letters, "JAPAN." $10.00 - $12.50

ROW 2:

1. Multi-flowers trimmed with gold, mark, in red letters, "7208," incised "W-90," paper label, "JAPAN." $15.00 - $20.00

2. Bird and pagoda, mark, in black letters, "MADE IN JAPAN." $60.00 - $80.00

3. Multi-flowers trimmed with gold, mark, in red letters, "7208," incised "W-90," paper label, "JAPAN."   Price per pair - $35.00 - $40.00

ROW 3:

1. Blue flowers, mark, in black letters, "MADE IN JAPAN." $12.50 - $17.50

2. Red and yellow flower, mark, in black letters, "MADE IN JAPAN." $15.00 - $20.00

3. Yellow flower, mark, incised, "MADE IN JAPAN." $12.50 - $17.50

86

Japan Miscellaneous

ROW 1:

1. Japanese woman, mark, incised, "MADE IN JAPAN." $45.00 - $60.00

2. Japanese woman, mark, paper label, "JAPAN," also written on back in pencil, (Love from mom 1956.) $20.00 - $25.00

ROW 2:

1. Man dancer trimmed with gold, mark, paper label, "JAPAN." $35.00 - $40.00

2. Woman dancer trimmed with gold, mark, paper label, "JAPAN." $35.00 - $40.00

Price per pair - $75.00 - $85.00

ROW 3:

1. Man, mark, in black letters, "MADE IN JAPAN." $35.00 - $40.00

2. Woman, mark, in black letters, "MADE IN JAPAN." $35.00 - $40.00

Price per pair - $75.00 - $85.00

Japan Miscellaneous

ROW 1:

1. Boy, brown hair, mark, in black letters, "MADE IN JAPAN." $15.00 - $20.00

2. Boy, blond hair, mark, in black letters, "MADE IN JAPAN." $15.00 - $20.00

3. Girl, blond hair, mark, in black letters, "MADE IN JAPAN." $15.00 - $20.00

   Above #1 and #3 price per pair - $35.00 - $45.00

ROW 2:

1. Boy with ball and dog, mark, in red letters, "JAPAN." $20.00 - $25.00

2. Dutch boy, mark, in red letters, "MADE IN JAPAN," and incised, "MADE IN JAPAN." $20.00 - $25.00

3. Boy with gun and dog, mark, in red letters, "MADE IN JAPAN." $20.00 - $25.00

ROW 3:

1. Dancing lady, mark, in black letters, "MADE IN JAPAN." $20.00 - $25.00

2. Woman standing, mark, in black letters, "JAPAN." $20.00 - $25.00

3. Dancing lady, mark, in black letters, "MADE IN JAPAN." Price per pair - $45.00 - $55.00

90

Japan Miscellaneous

ROW 1:

1. Outside scene and trimmed with gold, mark, paper label, "AUTHENTIC KASUGA WARE -JAPAN- HANDCRAFTED." $20.00 - $25.00

2. Outside scene and trimmed with gold, mark, paper label, "AUTHENTIC KASUGA WARE -JAPAN- HANDCRAFTED." $20.00 - $25.00

ROW 2:

1. Outside scene and trimmed with gold, mark, paper label, "AUTHENTIC KASUGA WARE -JAPAN- HANDCRAFTED." $20.00 - $25.00

2. Outside scene and trimmed with gold, mark, paper label, "AUTHENTIC KASUGA WARE -JAPAN- HANDCRAFTED." $20.00 - $25.00

   Price per set of four - $90.00 - $100.00

ROW 3

1. Green basket, mark, incised, "MADE IN JAPAN." $30.00 - $35.00

2. Flowers, mark, in black letters, "2811," paper label, "LEFTON'S REG US PAT OFF. EXCLUSIVES JAPAN." $15.00 - $20.00

Japan Miscellaneous

ROW 1:

1. Bird and flower, mark, paper label, "HAND PAINTED TILSO JAPAN," and in red letters, "53/355." $15.00 - $20.00

2. Multi-flowers, mark, incised, "MADE IN JAPAN." Also written on back in pencil (Xmas 1929.) $20.00 - $25.00

3. Bird and flower, mark, paper label, "HAND PAINTED TILSO JAPAN," and in red letters, "53/355."   Price per pair - $35.00 - $45.00

ROW 2:

1. Animal and trees, mark, in black letters, "MADE IN JAPAN." $15.00 - $20.00

2. White lily, mark, in black letters, "MARUHOM WARE (K) MADE IN JAPAN." $40.00 - $50.00

3. Duck playing violin, mark, in black letters, "MADE IN JAPAN." $15.00 - $20.00

ROW 3:

1. Girl and flowers, mark, in black letters, "MADE IN JAPAN." $20.00 - $25.00

2. Tulips, mark, incised, "MADE IN JAPAN." $40.00 - $50.00

3. Man and woman trimmed with gold, mark, in black letters, "HAND PAINTED (H) JAPAN." $35.00 - $40.00

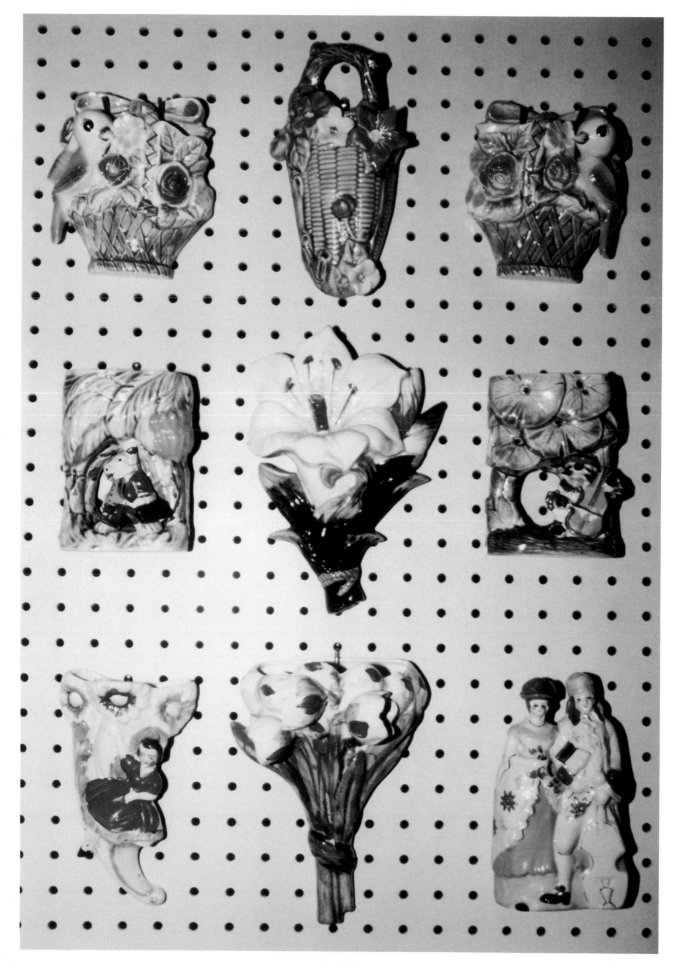

94

Japan Miscellaneous

ROW 1:

1. Cactus with red blossoms, mark, incised, "MADE IN JAPAN." $15.00 - $20.00

2. Mexican man sleeping, mark, in red letters, "JAPAN." $15.00 - $20.00

3. Cactus with yellow blossoms, mark, incised, "MADE IN JAPAN." $15.00 - $20.00

ROW 2:

1. Flower in pot, mark, incised, "MADE IN JAPAN." $15.00 - $20.00

2. Mexican playing guitar, mark, in black letters, "JAPAN." $15.00 - $20.00

3. "Mexican man, mark, in red letters, "JAPAN." $15.00 - $20.00

ROW 3:

1. Mexican woman, mark, in black letters, "MADE IN JAPAN." $15.00 - $20.00

2. Mexican man, mark, in black letters, "MADE IN JAPAN." $15.00 - $20.00

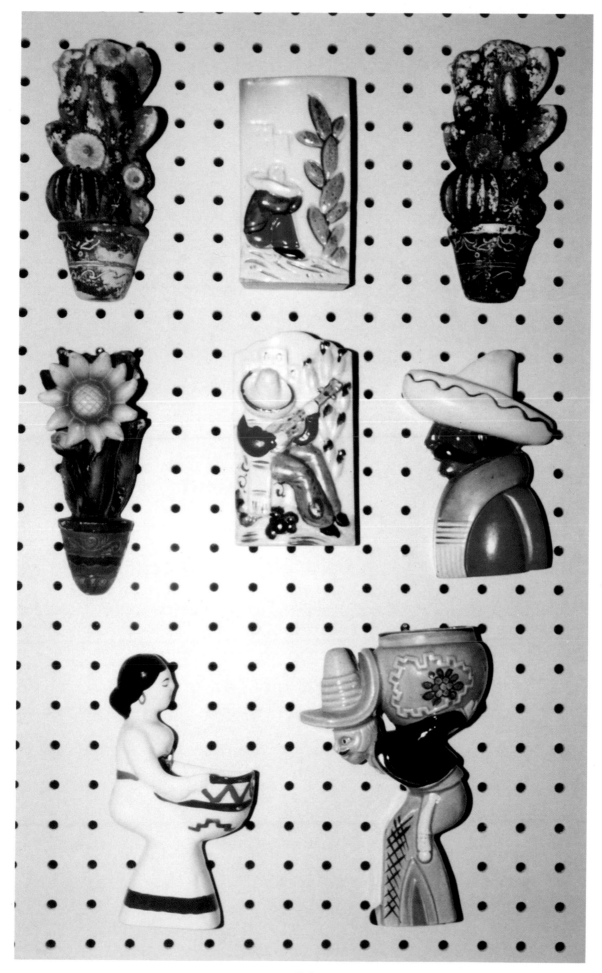

Japan Miscellaneous

ROW 1:

1. Little sunflower face, mark, in green letters, "MADE IN JAPAN." $10.00 - $15.00

2. Large sunflower face, mark, in green letters, "MADE IN JAPAN." $20.00 - $25.00

3. Little sunflower face, mark, in green letters, "MADE IN JAPAN." $10.00 - $15.00

Price per set of three - $45.00 - $60.00

ROW 2:

1. Blue hat, mark, in green letters, "MADE IN JAPAN HAND PAINTED." $15.00 - $20.00

2. Elf and flower, mark, in red letters, "HAND PAINTED ROYAL SEALY JAPAN." $15.00 - $20.00

3. Blue hat, mark, in green letters, "MADE IN JAPAN HAND PAINTED."   Price per pair - $35.00 - $45.00

ROW 3:

1. Violin with pansies and trimmed with gold, mark, paper label, "HAND PAINTED ROYAL JAPAN." $20.00 - $25.00

2. Violin with pink roses, mark, paper label, "JAPAN," and in green letters, "B2417." $15.00 - $20.00

3. Violin with pansies and cherries, mark, in black letters, "*JAPAN." Original price on back 47 cents. $10.00 - $15.00

Japan Miscellaneous

ROW 1:

1. Bird on limb, mark, incised, "MADE IN JAPAN." Original price on back 35 cents. $20.00 - $25.00

2. Bird and berries, mark, in black letters, "MADE IN JAPAN." $20.00 - $25.00

3. Parrot, orange, mark, in black letters, "MADE IN JAPAN*HAND PAINT." $20.00 - $25.00

ROW 2:

1. Bird and purple flowers, mark, incised, "MADE IN JAPAN." $25.00 - $35.00

2. Bird on limb, mark, incised, "MADE IN JAPAN." $30.00 - $40.00

3. Bird and purple flowers, mark, incised, "MADE IN JAPAN." Price per pair - $55.00 - $75.00

ROW 3:

1. Bird and mauve flower, mark, incised, "MADE IN JAPAN." $25.00 - $35.00

2. Bird and grapes, mark, in black letters, "MADE IN JAPAN." $20.00 - $30.00

3. Bird and mauve flower, mark, incised, "MADE IN JAPAN." Price per pair - $55.00 - $75.00

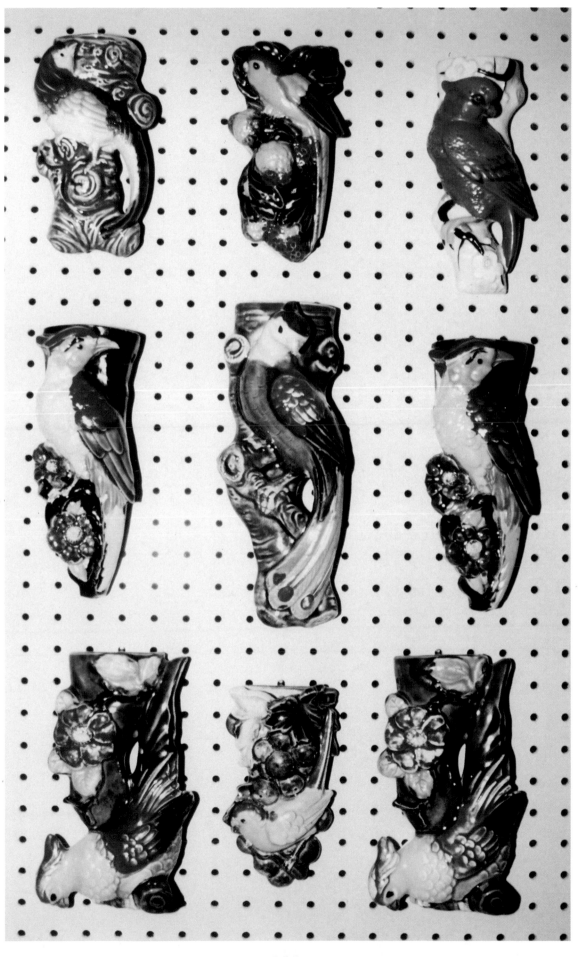

100

Japan Miscellaneous

ROW 1:

1. Bird on limb, mark, incised, "MADE IN JAPAN." $20.00 - $25.00

2. Bird, red, on limb, mark, in black letters, "MADE IN JAPAN." $20.00 - $30.00

3. Bird on limb, mark, incised, "MADE IN JAPAN." Original price on back 25 cents.
   Price per pair - $45.00 - $55.00

ROW 2:

1. Parrot, mauve, on limb, mark, incised, "MADE IN JAPAN." $20.00 - $25.00

2. Parrot, green, on limb, mark, incised, "MADE IN JAPAN." $25.00 - $30.00

3. Parrot, red, on limb, mark, incised, "MADE IN JAPAN." $20.00 - $25.00

ROW 3:

1. Parrot and mauve flowers, mark, incised, "MADE IN JAPAN," and in black letters, "MADE IN JAPAN." $20.00 - $25.00

2. Bird, green, and yellow flowers, mark, in black letters, "MADE IN JAPAN." $20.00 - $30.00

3. Parrot and mauve flowers, mark, incised, "MADE IN JAPAN." Original price on back 75 cents. Also marked (X-MAS 1929.)
   Price per pair - $45.00 - $55.00

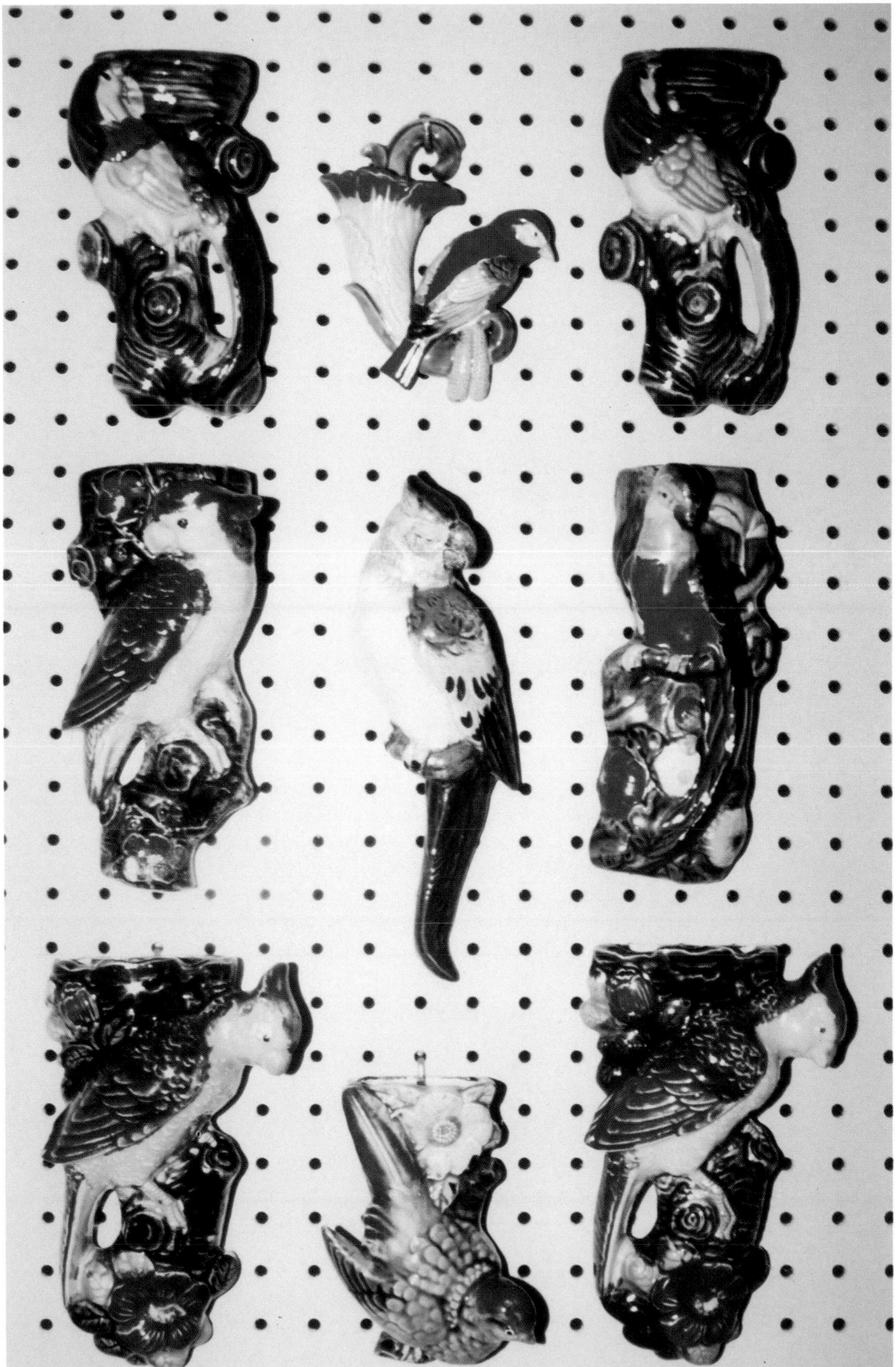

Japan Miscellaneous

ROW 1:

1. Bird on limb, mark, in black letters, "MADE IN JAPAN." $20.00 - $25.00

2. Bird, brown, on limb, mark, in black letters, "HAND PAINT*MADE IN JAPAN." $15.00 - $20.00

3. Bird on limb, mark, in black letters, "MADE IN JAPAN."   Price per pair - $45.00 - $55.00

ROW 2:

1. Parrot and red flower, mark, incised, "MADE IN JAPAN." $15.00 - $20.00

2. Parrot on limb with yellow berries, mark, in black letters, "MADE IN JAPAN." $20.00 - $30.00

3. Parrot, red and yellow flowers, mark, incised, "MADE IN JAPAN." Original price on back 10 cents. $15.00 - $20.00

ROW 3:

1. Bird on limb, red, white and yellow flowers, mark, incised, "MADE IN JAPAN." $20.00 - $25.00

2. Bird, green, on limb, mark, in red letters, "HAND PAINT*MADE IN JAPAN." $15.00 - $20.00

3. Bird on limb, pink, white and yellow flowers, mark, incised, "MADE IN JAPAN." Price per pair - $45.00 - $55.00

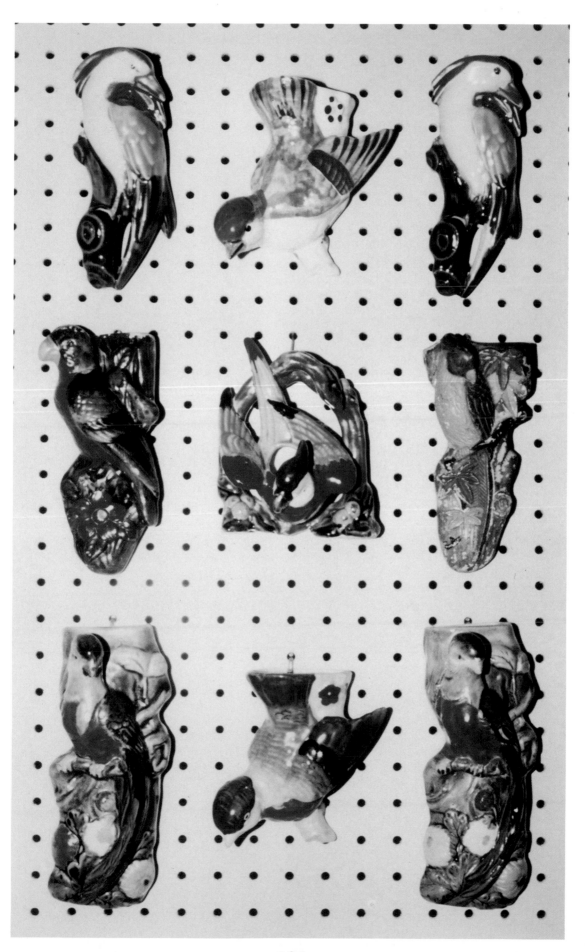

Japan Miscellaneous

ROW 1:

    1.   Rooster and hen, mark, incised, "MADE IN JAPAN." $25.00 - $35.00

    2.   Bird on perch, mark, incised, "MADE IN JAPAN." $25.00 - $30.00

ROW 2:

    1.   Owl on limb, mark, in black letters, "MADE IN JAPAN." $20.00 - $25.00

    2.   Owl, brown, mark, incised, "MADE IN JAPAN." Original price 50 cents. $20.00 - $25.00

    3.   Owl on limb, mark, incised, "MADE IN JAPAN." $45.00 - $55.00

ROW 3:

    1.   Rooster trimmed with gold, mark, paper label, "LIPPER & MANN CREATIONS JAPAN." $25.00 - $35.00

    2.   Rooster, mark, paper label, "AUTHENTIC KASUGA WARE JAPAN HANDCRAFTED." $20.00 - $30.00

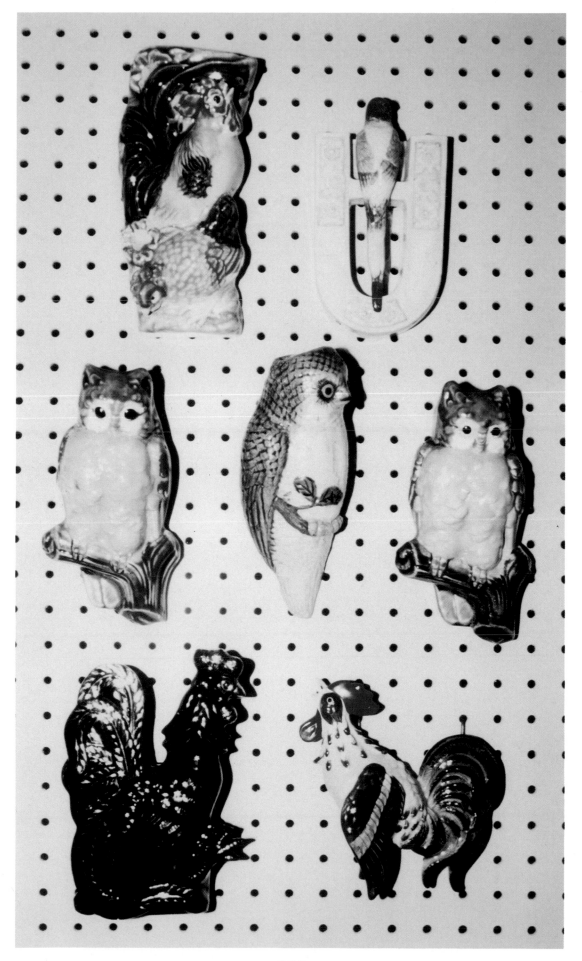

Japan Miscellaneous

ROW 1:

Blue Jay flying, mark, paper label, "A FAIRYLAND JAPAN." $20.00 - $30.00

ROW 2:

1. Birds and pink plate, mark, paper label, "JAPAN," and in black letters, "ORIOLE." $15.00 - $20.00

2. Bird and white plate, mark, paper label, "JAPAN," and "THAMES HAND PAINTED MADE IN JAPAN," and in black letters, "MYRTLE WARBLER." $15.00 - $20.00

ROW 3:

1. Bird feeding babies and red berries, mark, in black letters, "MYRTLE WARBLER." $10.00 - $15.00

2. Bird feeding babies and red apples, mark, paper label, "ORION JAPAN." $15.00 - $20.00

ROW 4:

Birds on blue, mark, paper label, "JAPAN." $10.00 - $15.00

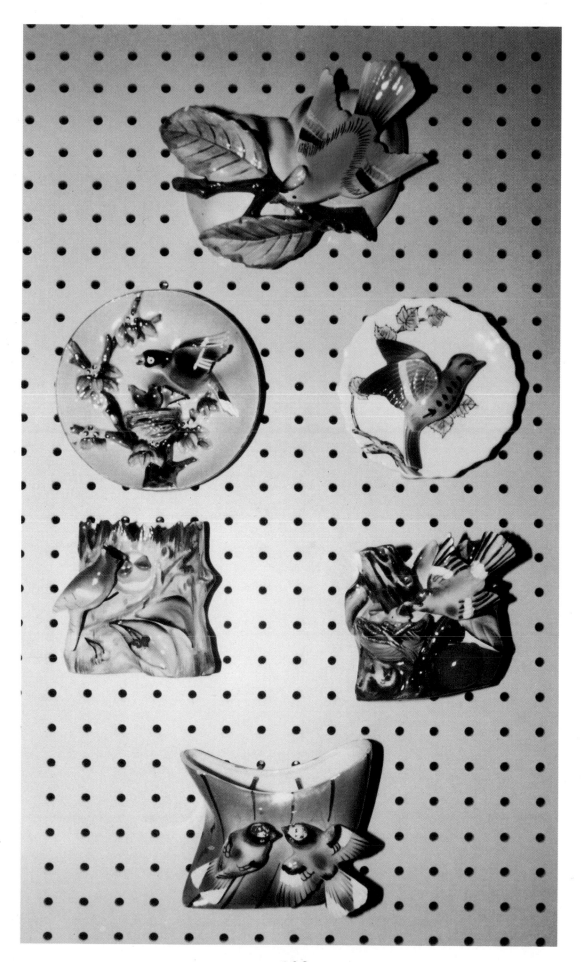

Japan Miscellaneous

ROW 1:

1.   Bird, pink, mark, paper label, "JAPAN." $10.00 - $15.00

2.   Bird on limb, mark, in black letters, "*JAPAN." $15.00 - $20.00

ROW 2:

1.   Bird and orange, mark, paper label, "SUPREME QUALITY T.M.J. JAPAN," and in black letters, "CARDINAL 3292." $15.00 - $20.00

2.   Bird on blue book, mark, paper label, "ENESCO IMPORTS JAPAN." $10.00 - $15.00

3.   Bird on limb, mark, paper label, "ENESCO IMPORTS JAPAN." $15.00 - $20.00

ROW 3:

1.   Bird with hat, mark, paper label, "JAPAN." $10.00 - $12.00

2.   Bird on limb, mark, paper label, "JAPAN," and in black letters, "W20." $10.00 - $12.00

3.   Swan, mark, paper label, "JAPAN." $10.00 - $12.00

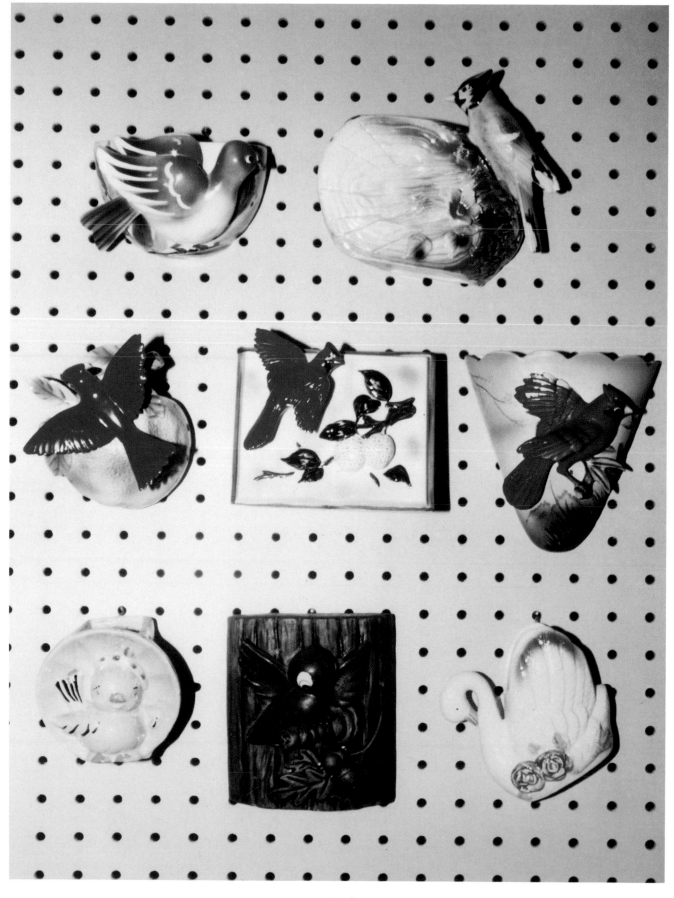

Japan Miscellaneous

ROW 1:
        Yellow duck, mark, paper label, "JAPAN." $15.00 - $17.00

ROW 2:
1.   Duck, white and yellow, mark, in black letters, $10.00 - $15.00
        "JAPAN."

2.   Duck, green, head, mark, in red letters, "JAPAN." $15.00 - $20.00

ROW 3:
1.   Duck in grass, mark, paper label, "JAPAN." $10.00 - $15.00

112

Japan Miscellaneous

ROW 1:

1. Duck, green head, large size, mark, paper label, "UCAGCO CERAMICS JAPAN." $12.00 - $15.00

2. Duck, green head, large size, mark, paper label, "UCAGCO CERAMICS JAPAN."   Price per pair - $25.00 - $35.00

ROW 2:

1. Duck, green head, medium size, mark, paper label, "UCAGCO CERAMICS JAPAN." $10.00 - $12.00

2. Duck, green head, medium size, mark, paper label, "UCAGCO CERAMICS JAPAN."
Price per pair - $22.00 - $27.00

ROW 3:

1. Duck, green head, small size, mark, paper label, "UCAGCO CERAMICS JAPAN." $7.00 - $10.00

2. Duck, green head, small size, mark, paper label, "UCAGCO CERAMICS JAPAN."   Price per pair - $15.00 - $25.00

The above ducks can also be bought as a set of three, which includes, one large, one medium and one small. $30.00 - $40.00

ROW 4:

Flying duck, mark, paper label, "NORCREST FINE CHINA JAPAN." $15.00 - $20.00

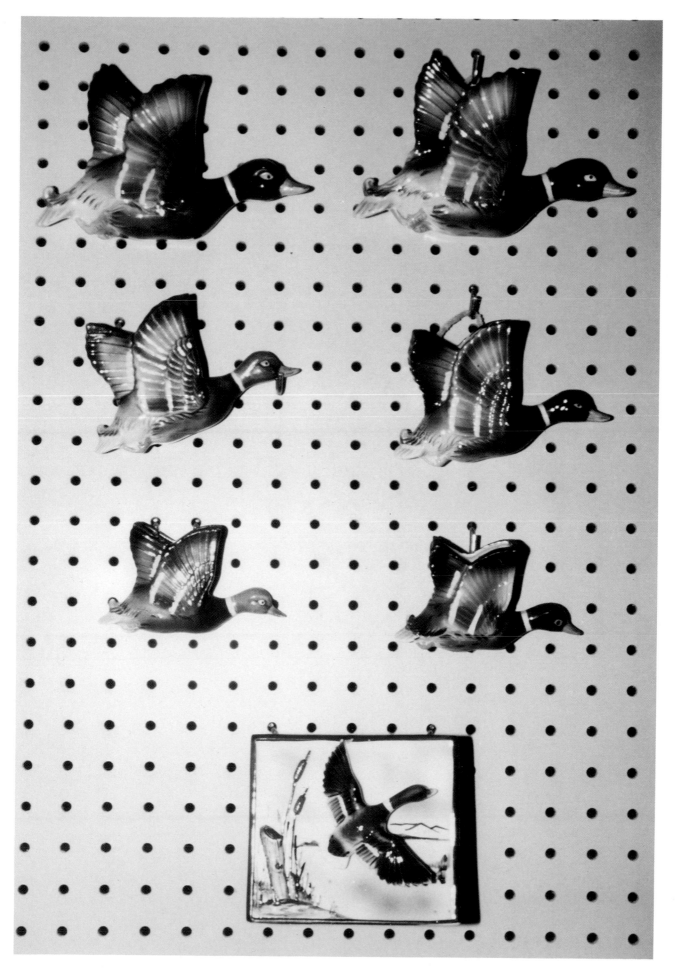

Japan Miscellaneous

ROW 1:

Duck, green head, small size, mark, paper label, $12.00 - $15.00
"JAPAN."

ROW 2:

Duck, green head, medium size, mark, paper label, $15.00 - $20.00
"JAPAN."

Price per pair - $30.00 - $37.00

ROW 3:

Big duck, green head, mark, paper label, "CHASE $15.00 - $20.00
JAPAN." The way the holes are in the back side,
it makes the duck fly straight up.

ROW 4:

Big duck, green head, mark, paper label, "CHASE $15.00 - $20.00
JAPAN."

Ducks in rows #3 and #4, Price per pair - $32.00 - $45.00

116

Japan Miscellaneous

ROW 1:

Duck, green head, large size, mark, paper label, "UCAGCO CERAMICS JAPAN." $12.00 - $15.00

ROW 2:

1. Duck, green head, large size, mark, paper label, "UCAGCO CERAMICS JAPAN." $12.00 - $15.00

2. Duck, green head, medium size, mark, paper label, "UCAGCO CERAMICS JAPAN." $10.00 - $12.00

ROW 3:

1. Duck, green head, large size, mark, paper label, "UCAGCO CERAMICS JAPAN." $12.00 - $15.00

2. Duck, green head, medium size, mark, paper label, "UCAGCO CERAMICS JAPAN." $10.00 - $12.00

ROW 4:

1. Duck, green head, small size, mark, paper label, "UCAGCO CERAMICS JAPAN." $7.00 - $10.00

The above ducks can also be bought as a set of three which includes, one large, one medium and one small. $30.00 - $40.00

ROW 5:

Hunting dog with duck, mark, paper label, "JAPAN," and in green letters, "B3872." $10.00 - $12.00

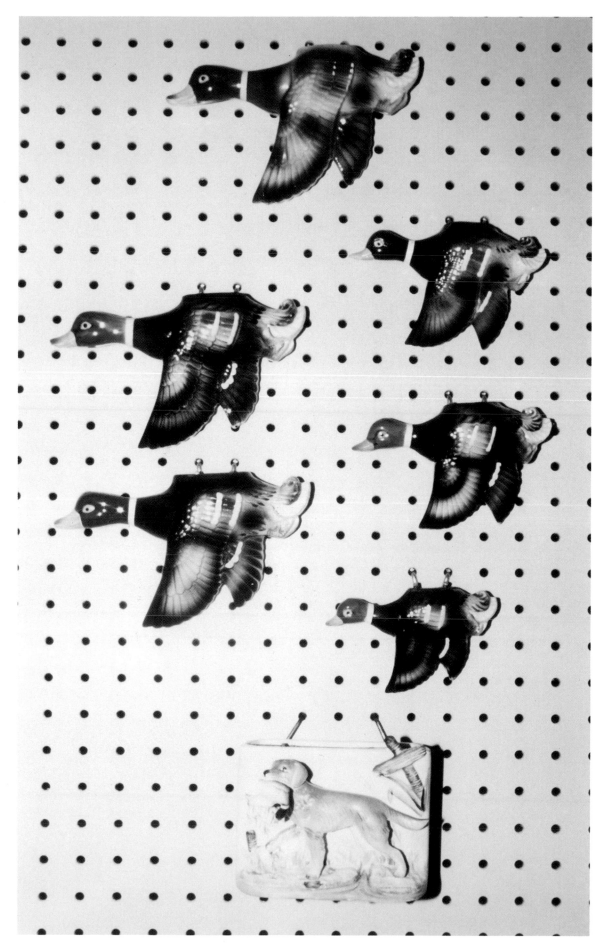

Japan Miscellaneous

ROW 1:

1. Strawberry, mark, in black letters, "MADE IN JAPAN." $15.00 - $20.00

2. Pear, mark, in black letters, "MADE IN JAPAN." $15.00 - $20.00

3. Peach, mark, in black letters, "MADE IN JAPAN." $15.00 - $20.00

ROW 2:

1. Apples, mark, paper label, "JAPAN." $15.00 - $20.00

2. Grapes, mark, incised, "MADE IN JAPAN," and in black letters, "MADE IN JAPAN." $15.00 - $20.00

3. Bananas, mark, paper label, "MADE IN JAPAN." Original price on back 39 cents. $15.00 - $20.00

ROW 3:

1. Apples on plate, mark, in green letters, "MADE IN JAPAN HAND PAINTED." $25.00 - $35.00

2. Apples on plate, mark, in green letters, "MADE IN JAPAN HAND PAINTED."   Price per pair - $55.00 - $75.00

ROW 4:

1. Pears, mark, paper labels, "JAPAN," and "KRESS." $10.00 - $15.00

2. Grapes, mark, paper label, "LEFTON EXCLUSIVE JAPAN." $15.00 - $20.00

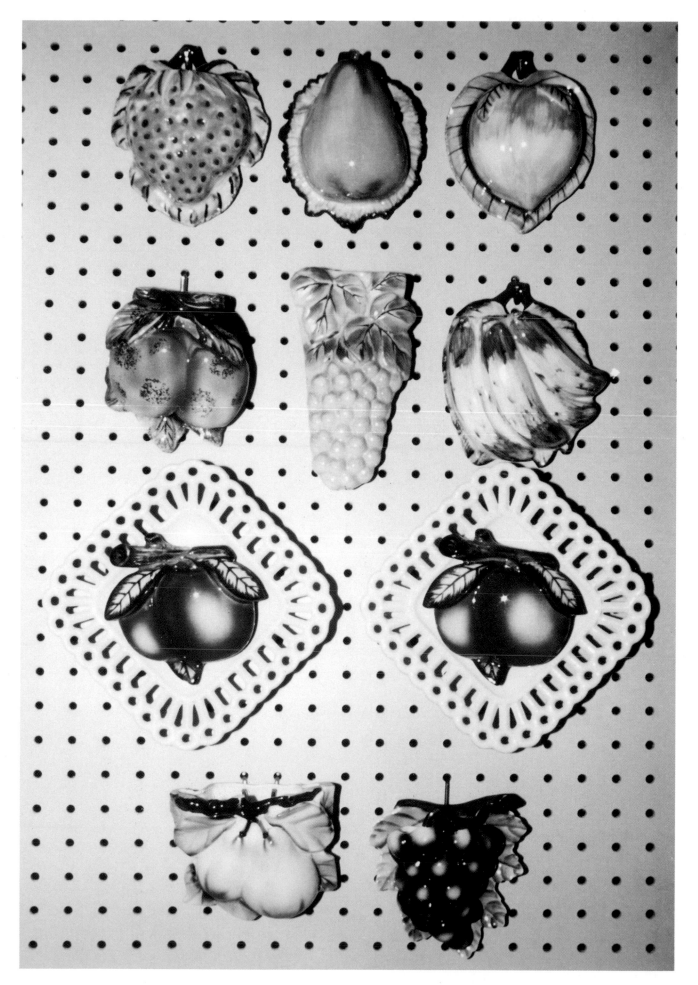

Japan Miscellaneous

ROW 1:

1. House, mark, paper label, "JAPAN, " and in black letters, "7529." $10.00 - $15.00

2. Elf, mark, paper label, "IMPORT JAPAN." $10.00 - $12.00

ROW 2:

1. House with tower, mark, paper label, "MADE IN JAPAN COUNTERPOINT SAN FRANCISCO 94103-R." $10.00 - $12.00

2. House with snow, mark, paper label, "JAPAN." $10.00 - $12.00

3. House, flat roof, mark, paper label, "MADE IN JAPAN COUNTERPOINT SAN FRANCISCO 94103-R." $10.00 - $12.00

ROW 3:

1. Fireplace, pink, mark, paper label, "JAPAN." $10.00 - $15.00

2. Fireplace, brown, mark, paper label, "TILSO JAPAN." $10.00 - $15.00

Japan Miscellaneous

ROW 1:

1. Birds on book, trimmed with gold, mark, in red letters, "JAPAN." $10.00 - $12.00

2. Mary, trimmed with gold, mark, in black letters, "© GEO. Z. LEFTON 1956-502778," and paper label, "JAPAN." $15.00 - $20.00

3. Bird and flowers on book, trimmed with gold, mark paper label, "JAPAN," and red letters, "52/631." $10.00 - $12.00

ROW 2:

1. Cross, pink base, trimmed with gold, mark, in gold letters, "E-563," and paper label, "REG. US. PAT. OFF. NORCREST JAPAN." $10.00 - $15.00

2. Violin, trimmed with gold, mark, paper label, "SONSCO JAPAN." $15.00 - $20.00

3. Cross, blue base, trimmed with gold, mark, in gold letters, "E-563," and paper label, REG. US. PAT. OFF. NORCREST JAPAN." $10.00 - $15.00

ROW 3:

1. Bird on book, trimmed with gold, mark, paper label, "A QUALITY PRODUCT JAPAN." $10.00 - $12.00

2. Cross, trimmed with gold, mark, paper label, "REG. US. PAT. OFF. NORCREST JAPAN," and in gold letters, "X-102." Original price on back $2.00. $10.00 - $15.00

3. Flowers on book, trimmed with gold, mark, paper label, "LUGENE'S JAPAN." $10.00 - $12.00

ROW 4:

1. Angel dressed in black robe. $20.00 - $25.00

2. Angel dressed in pink robe. $20.00 - $25.00

3. Angel dressed in yellow robe. $10.00 - $25.00

The angels are all marked the same, in black letters, "K1717," and paper label, "NAPCO JAPAN."

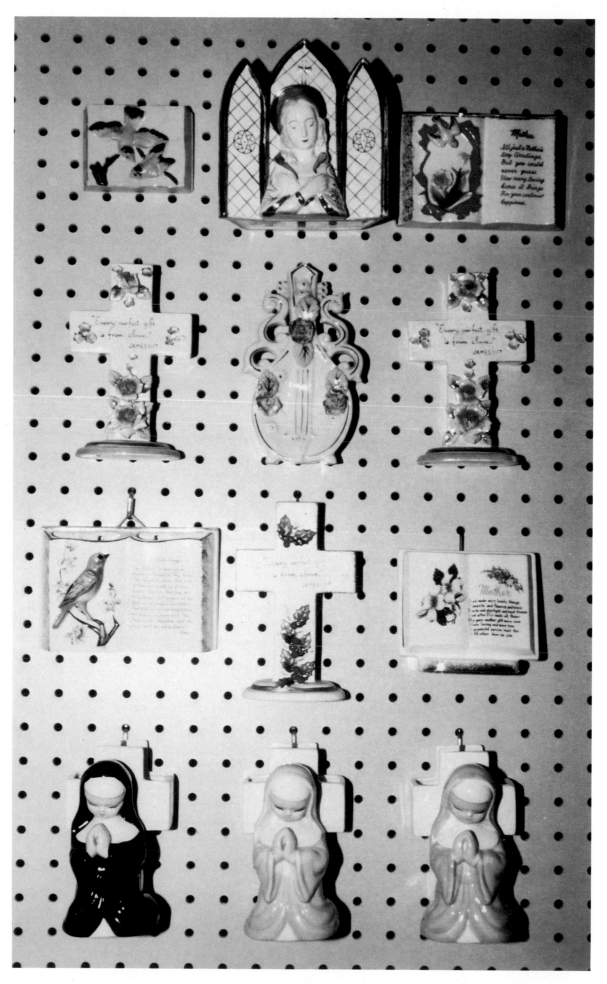

Japan Miscellaneous

ROW 1:

1. Ship going right, trimmed with gold, mark, incised, "JAPAN," and in red letters, "MADE IN JAPAN-MM." $15.00 - $20.00

2. Ship with part luster finish, mark, in red letters, "HAND PAINT TT MADE IN JAPAN." $25.00 - $30.00

3. Ship going left, trimmed with gold, mark, incised, "JAPAN," and in red letters, "MADE IN JAPAN MM." $15.00 - $20.00

ROW 2:

1. Ship with brown flying bird, mark, incised, "MADE IN JAPAN," and in black letters, "MADE IN JAPAN." $15.00 - $20.00

2. Ship with red sails, two anchors hanging down on strings, mark, in red letters, "PAT NO 64211 MADE IN JAPAN." $20.00 - $25.00

3. Ship with black flying bird, mark, incised, "MADE IN JAPAN," and in black letters, "MADE IN JAPAN." $15.00 - $20.00

ROW 3:

1. Sea shell trimmed with gold, mark, paper label, "IMPORTS ENESCO JAPAN." $15.00 - $20.00

2. Sea shell trimmed with gold, mark, paper label, "IMPORTS ENESCO JAPAN." Price per pair - $32.00 - $45.00

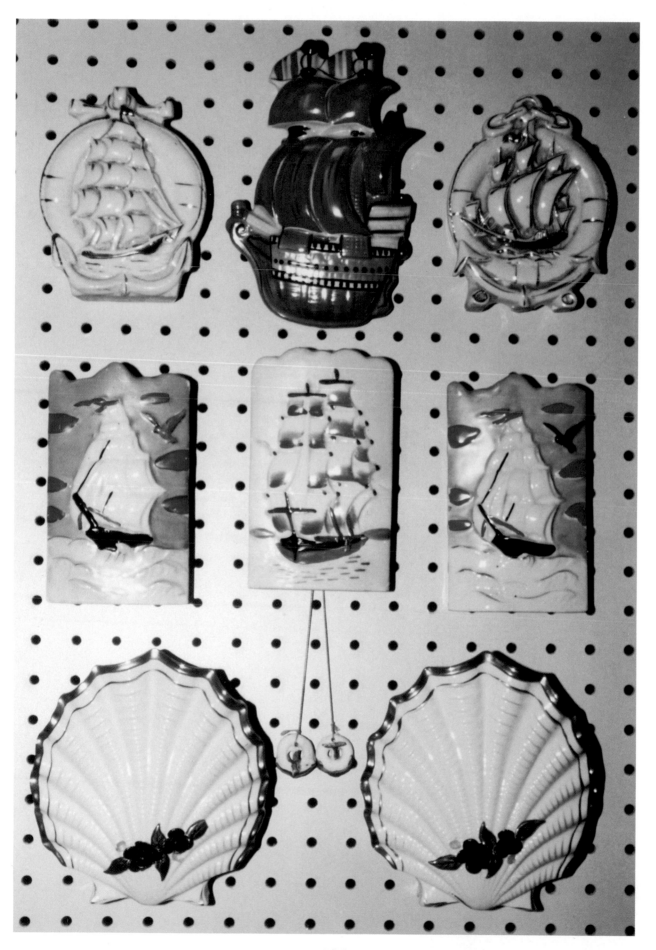

126

Japan Miscellaneous

ROW 1:

1. Horse heads, mark, paper label, "JAPAN." Original price on back 78 cents. $15.00 - $20.00

2. Deer, mark, in red letters, "JAPAN," and incised, "JAPAN." $15.00 - $20.00

3. Horse head, mark, in black letters, "JAPAN." $15.00 - $20.00

ROW 2:

1. Horse heads, mark, paper label, "JAPAN." $20.00 - $30.00

2. Cow, mark, in red letters, "JAPAN." $15.00 - $20.00

ROW 3:

1. Dog, mark, incised, "JAPAN," and in black letters, "MADE IN JAPAN." $15.00 - $25.00

2. Horse head, mark, in black letters, "JAPAN." $15.00 - $20.00

3. Jockey on horse, mark, in black letters, "MADE IN JAPAN," and incised, "MADE IN JAPAN." $15.00 - $20.00

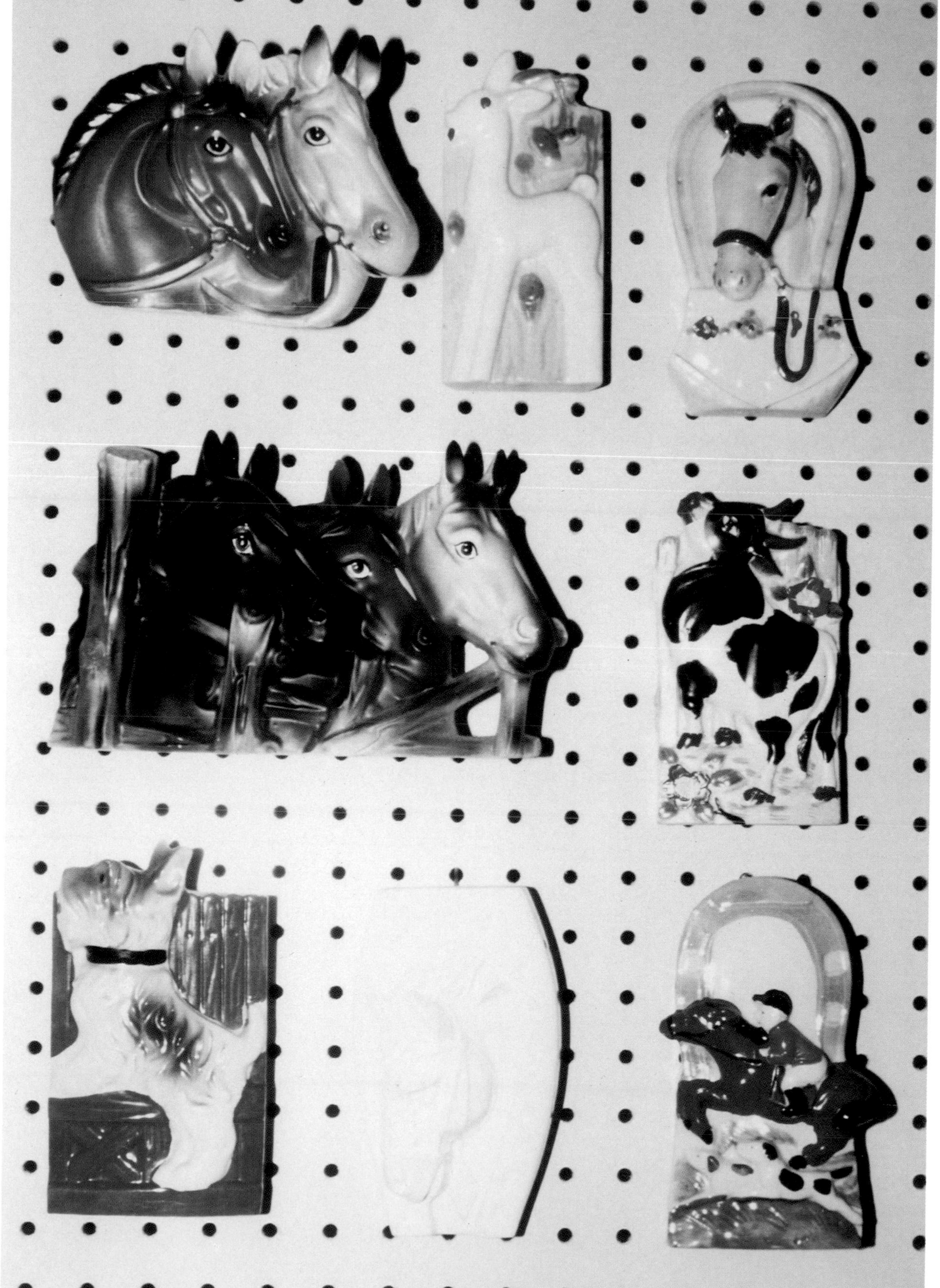

Japan Miscellaneous

ROW 1:

1. Penguin, mark, in black letters, "4416," and paper label, "STYLED BY SHAFFORD JAPAN." $10.00 - $12.00

2. Shoe, mark, in red letters, "RAGGEDY ANN AND ANDY ©TM 1976 THE BOBBS-MERRILL CO. INC., RUBENS ORIGINALS LOS ANGELES, CALIF. 90021 INC. JAPAN." $20.00 - $25.00

3. Car, mark, paper label, "JAPAN," and incised, "#355." $10.00 - $15.00

ROW 2:

1. Girl with ball, mark, paper label, "JAPAN," and in black letters, "4415." $10.00 - $12.00

2. Girl and rabbit, mark, in black letters, "39/2," and paper label, "LIPPER & MANN CREATIONS JAPAN." $15.00 - $20.00

3. Dog, mark, in black letters "MADE IN JAPAN." $10.00 - $12.00

ROW 3:

1. Donkey and cart, mark, paper label, "JAPAN." $15.00 - $20.00

2. Girl in swing, mark, in black letters, "JAPAN." $10.00 - $12.00

3. Baby in diaper, mark, in black letters, "4921," and paper label, "JAPAN." $10.00 - $12.00

Japan Miscellaneous

ROW 1:

1. 50th anniversary, trimmed with gold, mark, in black letters, "E2293," and paper label, "IMPORTS ENESCO JAPAN." $10.00 - $15.00

2. 25th anniversary, trimmed with silver, mark, paper label, "ART LINE AL JAPAN." $10.00 - $15.00

ROW 2:

1. Pink fish, mark, in black letters, "JAPAN." $15.00 - $20.00

2. Fish creel with flys, mark, in black letters, K3186," and paper label, "A NAPCO CERAMIC JAPAN." $10.00 - $12.00

3. Green fish, mark in black letters, "MADE IN JAPAN." $15.00 - $20.00

ROW 3:

1. Wisconsin hearts, mark, in black letters, "MADE IN JAPAN." Original price $1.00. $10.00 - $15.00

2. Scene, blue, mark, in black letters, "PARK CROWN JAPAN HAND DECORATED," and paper label, "HAND PAINTED." $5.00 - $7.50

3. Yellow filter basket, mark, in green letters, "SIGMA©MCMLXXXIV," and paper label, "MADE IN JAPAN." $10.00 - $15.00

Japan Miscellaneous

ROW 1:

1. Christmas singers trimmed with gold, mark, in black letters, "JAPAN." $10.00 - $15.00

2. Christmas deer trimmed with gold, mark in black letters, "MOUNT CLEMENS POTTERY MADE IN JAPAN." $10.00 - $12.00

ROW 2:

1. Dutch windmill, mark, in black letters, "370," and paper label, "JAPAN." $10.00 - $15.00

2. Kitchen stove, mark, in black letters, "374." $10.00 - $15.00

3. Clock, mark, in black letters, "372." Note, all three wall pockets in above row 2 have the same fruit pattern. $10.00 - $15.00

ROW 3:

1. Blue heating stove, mark, in black letters, "3P158," and paper labels, "JAPAN," and "SONSCO JAPAN." $10.00 - $15.00

2. Blue heating stove, mark, in black letters, "3P158," and paper labels, "JAPAN," and "SONSCO JAPAN."   Price per pair - These also have the fruit pattern. $22.00 - $35.00

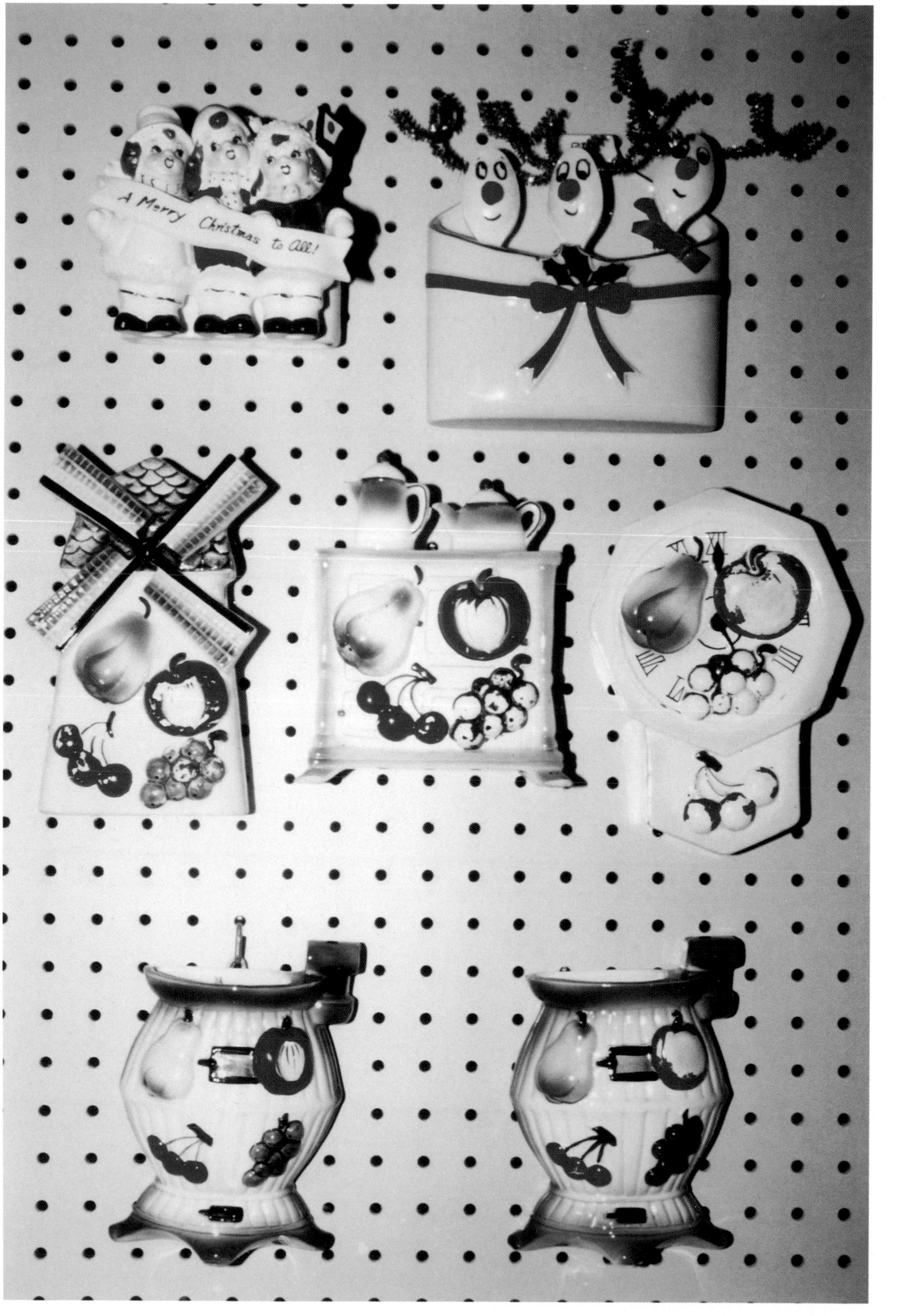
A Merry Christmas to All!

Japan Miscellaneous

ROW 1:

Spice rack, mark, in black letters, "JAPAN." $10.00 - $15.00

ROW 2:

1. Cup and plate trimmed with pink, mark, paper label, "FREDROBERTS COMPANY CHINA SAN FRANCISCO MADE IN JAPAN." $20.00 - $25.00

2. Cup and plate trimmed with green, mark, paper label "FREDROBERTS COMPANY CHINA SAN FRANCISCO MADE IN JAPAN." $20.00 - $25.00

ROW 3:

1. Skillet, mark, in black letters, "3850," and paper label, "LEFTON'S REG. US. PAT. OFF. EXCLUSIVES JAPAN." $10.00 - $15.00

2. Dust pan, green. $10.00 - $15.00

ROW 4:

1. Fruit in basket with handle, mark, paper label, "JAPAN." $15.00 - $20.00

2. Fruit in basket, mark, paper label, "MADE IN JAPAN." $15.00 - $20.00

136

Japan Miscellaneous

ROW 1:

1. Sprinkler, mark, paper label, "JAPAN," and in black letters, "S727R." $10.00 - $12.00

2. Chef, mark, paper label, "JAPAN." $25.00 - $30.00

3. Sprinkler, mark, paper label, "JAPAN," and in black letters, "S727R."   Price per pair - $22.00 - $25.00

ROW 2:

1. Teapot, tan, mark, paper label, "JAPAN." $10.00 - $15.00

2. Tea kettle, white, mark, paper labels, "JAPAN," and "A LORRIE * DESIGN." $15.00 - $20.00

ROW 3:

1. Bowl with fruit, mark, paper label, "LEFTON'S REG. US. PAT. OFF. EXCLUSIVES JAPAN," and in black letters," GEO. Z. LEFTON #4379." $5.00 - $7.00

2. Plate with apples, mark, paper label, "MADE IN THAME JAPAN." $15.00 - $20.00

3. Bowl with fruit, mark, paper label, "LEFTON'S REG. US. PAT. OFF. EXCLUSIVES JAPAN," and in black letters," GEO. Z. LEFTON #4379."   Price per pair - $12.00 - $15.00

ROW 4:

1. Pitcher, trimmed with gold, mark, paper label, "JAPAN," and in red letters, "E2366OMC." $10.00 - $15.00

2. Pitcher, white, mark, paper label, "ARDCO FINE QUALITY DALLAS MADE IN JAPAN." $15.00 - $20.00

3. Cup and saucer, mark, in red letters, "MADE IN JAPAN." $15.00 - $20.00

138

Japan Miscellaneous

ROW 1:

Tea kettle with spice hangers, mark, paper label, "JAPAN." — $20.00 - $25.00

ROW 2:

1. Cup and saucer with slots to hang spoons from, mark, paper label, "FREDROBERTS COMPANY SAN FRANCISCO MADE IN JAPAN." — $10.00 - $15.00

2. Rolling pin, mark, paper label, "JAPAN," and in black letters, "221." — $10.00 - $15.00

ROW 3:

1. Skillet trimmed with green, mark, in black letters, "881," and paper label, "ARTMARK CHICAGO ILL. MADE IN JAPAN." — $10.00 - $15.00

2. Billows, mark, paper label, "FERN IMPORTAN HAND PAINTED JAPAN." — $10.00 - $15.00

3. Skillet trimmed with pink, mark, paper label, "ARTMARK CHICAGO ILL. MADE IN JAPAN." — $10.00 - $15.00

ROW 4:

1. Cup, mark, in green letters, "MORIKIN M JAPAN." Handle on left hand side. — $15.00 - $20.00

2. Billows, mark, in black letters, "P707," and paper label, "REG. US. PAT. OFF. NORCREST JAPAN." — $10.00 - $15.00

3. Cup, mark, in green letters, "MORIKIN M JAPAN." Handle on right hand side. — $15.00 - $20.00

Price per pair - $35.00 - $45.00

140

Japan Miscellaneous

ROW 1:

1. Pitcher trimmed with gold, mark, in red letters, "E2365," and paper label, "IMPORTS ENESCO JAPAN." Handle on left. $10.00 - $15.00

2. Tea kettle, mark, paper label, "JAPAN," and in black letters, "S727F." $10.00 - $15.00

3. Pitcher trimmed with gold, mark, in red letters, "E2365," and paper label, "IMPORTS ENESCO JAPAN." Handle on right. $10.00 - $15.00

   Price per pair - $25.00 - $35.00

ROW 2:

1. Pitcher, white, mark, in black letters, "2118W," and paper label, "LEFTON'S REG. US. PAT. OFF. EXCLUSIVES JAPAN." Handle on left. $15.00 - $20.00

2. Pitcher, brown, mark, in black letters, "JAPAN." $15.00 - $20.00

3. Pitcher, white, mark, in black letters, "2118W," and paper label, "LEFTON'S REG. US. PAT. OFF. EXCLUSIVES JAPAN." Handle on right. $15.00 - $20.00

   Price per pair - $35.00 - $45.00

ROW 3:

1. Pitcher, white, mark, paper label, "NAPCOWARE (N) MADE IN JAPAN," and in black letters, "8810." Handle on left. $15.00 - $20.00

2. Teapot with flowers, mark, paper label, "JAPAN," and in black letters, "3120." $10.00 - $15.00

3. Pitcher, white, mark, paper label, "NAPCOWARE (N) MADE IN JAPAN," and in black letters, "8810." Handle on right. $15.00 - $20.00

   Price per pair - $35.00 - $45.00

Japan Miscellaneous

ROW 1:

1. Green owl clock set at "8 o'clock." Mark in black letters, "JAPAN." $15.00 - $20.00

2. Green clock set at "12:25," mark, incised, "JAPAN," and paper label, "HAND PAINTED TILSO JAPAN." $20.00 - $25.00

3. Blue owl clock set at "8 o'clock." Mark, paper label, "HAND PAINTED ATLAS JAPAN." $15.00 - $20.00

ROW 2:

1. Dutch windmill clock set at "12:25" The pendulums are a small pair of Dutch shoes. The back is marked with a paper label, "HAND PAINTED TILSO JAPAN." $20.00 - $30.00

2. Clock, face is marked, "MONDAY THRU SUNDAY." The hand can be pointed to any day you want it on. Also printed on the base of clock is "REMEMBER TO WATER ON DAY INDICATED." The back is marked with paper label, "IMPORTS ENESCO JAPAN." $20.00 - $30.00

Japan Miscellaneous

ROW 1:

1. Small clock, no pendulums and set at "2 o'clock," mark, incised, "4137 MADE IN JAPAN." $5.00 - $7.00

2. Small clock with pendulums and set at "2 o'clock," mark, incised, "4137 MADE IN JAPAN." $6.00 - $8.00

3. Small clock with pendulums and set at "2 o'clock," mark, incised, "+," and in black letters, "JAPAN." $6.00 - $8.00

ROW 2:

1. Clock with pendulums and set at "12:46," mark, incised, "JAPAN." $15.00 - $20.00

2. Clock with pendulums and set at "11:05," mark in black letters, "8258 X Japan." $10.00 - $15.00

ROW 3:

1. Clock, no pendulums and set at "2:05," mark, incised, "MADE IN JAPAN," and in red letters, "MADE IN JAPAN." $8.00 - $10.00

2. Clock with pendulums and set at "2:05," mark, incised, "4134 JAPAN," and in red letters, "PAT. NO 64211 MADE IN JAPAN." $10.00 - $12.00

3. Clock, no pendulums and set at "2:05," mark, incised, "4134 MADE IN JAPAN," and in red letters, "JAPAN." $8.00 - $10.00

146

Japan Miscellaneous

ROW 1:

1.   Girl's head, mark, paper label, "JAPAN." $25.00 - $30.00

2.   Lady and rose, mark, incised, "MADE IN JAPAN," and in black letters, "MADE IN JAPAN." $25.00 - $30.00

3.   Boy's head, mark, paper label, "JAPAN." $20.00 - $25.00

ROW 2:

1.   Multi-color flowers trimmed with gold, mark, incised, "W-92," and in red letters, "MADE IN JAPAN." $15.00 - $20.00

2.   Owl and flowers, mark, incised, "MADE IN JAPAN." $20.00 - $30.00

3.   Grapes and flowers, mark, in black letters, "JAPAN." $15.00 - $20.00

ROW 3:

1.   Lady with ram heads, mark, incised, "MADE IN JAPAN." $15.00 - $20.00

2.   Fruit and leaves, mark, in black letters, "MADE IN JAPAN+." $20.00 - $30.00

3.   Lady with ram heads, mark, incised, "MADE IN JAPAN."   Price per pair - $35.00 - $45.00

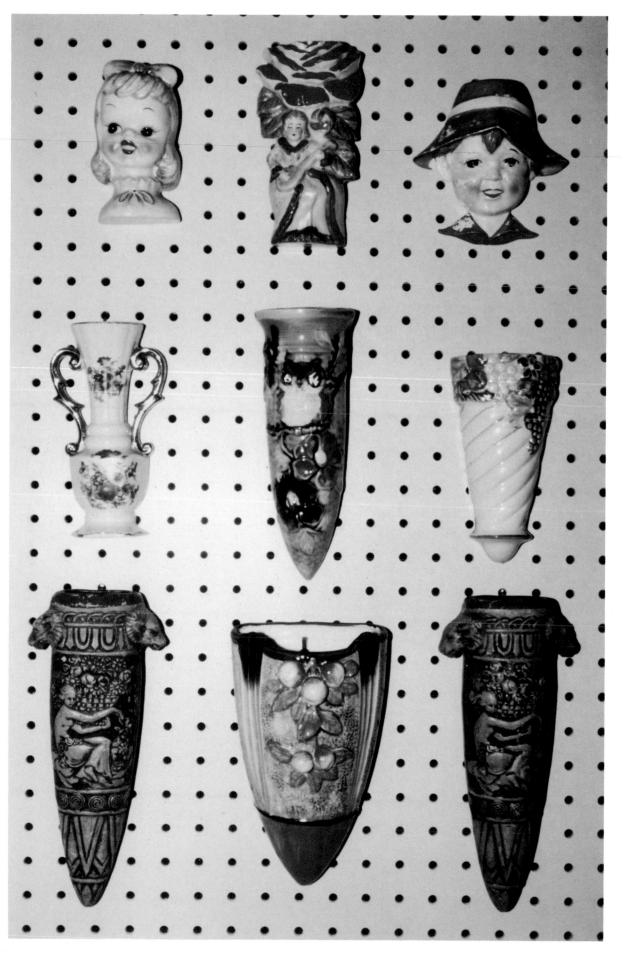

148

Japan Miscellaneous

ROW 1:

1. Hat with flowers, trimmed with gold and pearls, mark, incised, "G507," and paper label, "HAND PAINTED TILSO JAPAN." $20.00 - $25.00

2. Flying bird, mark, paper label, "JAPAN," and in black letters "WAXWING." $15.00 - $20.00

ROW 2:

1. Boy and girl with apples, mark, in blue letters, "JAPAN." $15.00 - $20.00

2. Boy and girl with basket, mark, in blue letters, "JAPAN." $15.00 - $20.00

ROW 3:

1. Hearts and (NEW MEXICO), mark, in black letters, "MADE IN JAPAN." $10.00 - $15.00

2. Dogs and dog house, mark, in black letters, "MADE IN JAPAN." $12.00 - $15.00

ROW 4:

1. Stove with fruit, mark, paper label, "MADE IN JAPAN," and in black letters, "373." $12.00 - $15.00

2. Fruit, mark, paper label, "JAPAN." $15.00 - $20.00

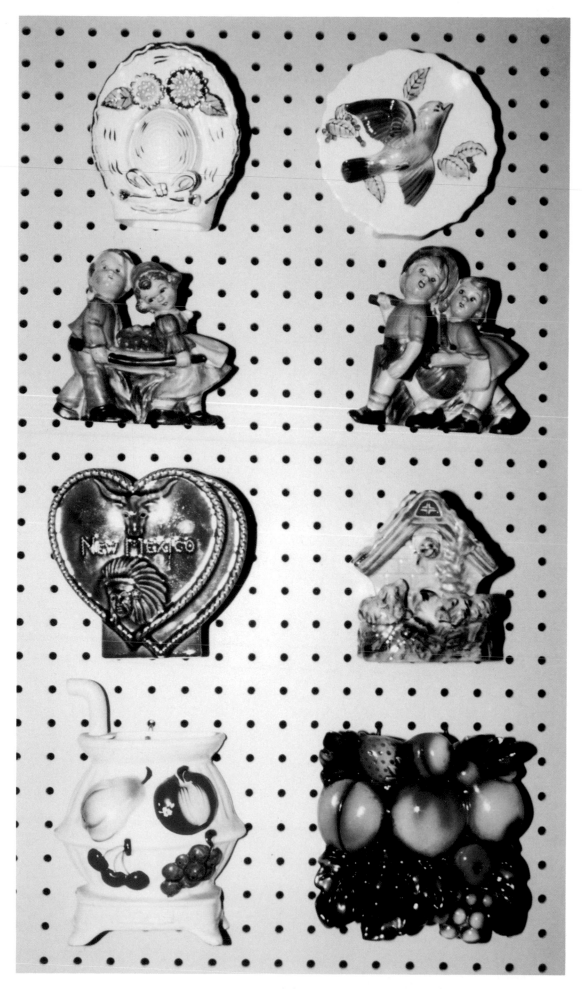

McCoy Pottery

McCoy Pottery started in Roseville, Ohio in 1910, making many great products of which their wall pockets are some of the finest. By the mid 1980's they closed, selling out to a New Jersey company. Hearsay has it they are using the original McCoy molds.

ROW 1:

1. Bird on pink flower, mark, "McCOY." Made in 1948. $30.00 - $35.00

2. Lily, yellow, mark, "McCOY." Made in 1948. $30.00 - $35.00

3. Bird on green bird bath, mark, "McCOY U.S.A." Made in 1949. $35.00 - $40.00

ROW 2:

1. Fan, blue, mark, "McCOY U.S.A." Made in 1956. $30.00 - $35.00

2. Teapot clock, blue, no mark. Made in 1952. $15.00 - $20.00

ROW 3:

1. Purple grapes, no mark. Made in 1953. $35.00 - $40.00

2. Pear, no mark. Made in 1953. Original price stamped on back, 69 cents. $30.00 - $35.00

ROW 4:

1. Diaper, green, mark, "837-USA." $20.00 - $25.00

2. Diaper, pink, mark "837-USA." $20.00 - $25.00

McCoy Pottery

ROW 1:

1. Umbrella, gold brocade, mark, "GOLD 24K McCOY USA." $35.00 - $40.00

2. Lady, white, mark, "McCOY." Made in 1943. $35.00 - $40.00

3. Umbrella, gold brocade, mark, "GOLD 24K McCoy USA."   Price per pair - $75.00 - $85.00

ROW 2:

1. Yellow flower, no mark. Made in 1946. $15.00 - $20.00

2. Owls on trivet, mark, "McCOY." Made in 1953. $35.00 - $40.00

ROW 3:

1. Umbrella, black, mark, "McCOY U.S.A." Made in 1957. Original price stamped on back is 59 cents. $25.00 - $30.00

2. Clown, white, mark, "McCoy." $30.00 - $35.00

3. Umbrella, black, mark, "McCOY U.S.A." Made in 1957. Original price stamped on back is 59 cents.   Price per pair - $55.00 - $65.00

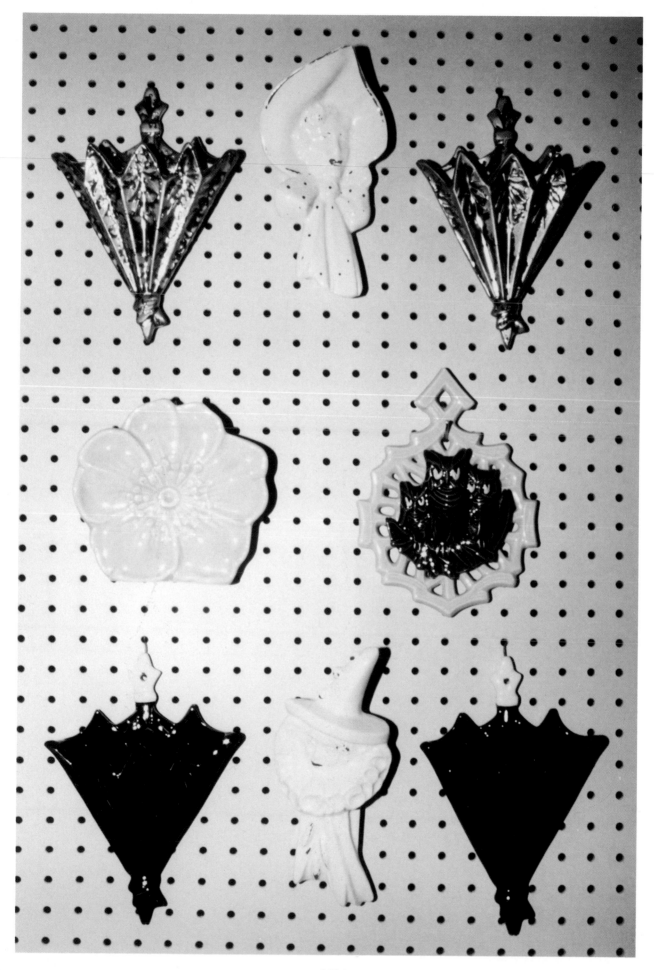

154

McCoy Pottery

ROW 1:

    1.   Blue flower, no mark. Made in 1946. $15.00 - $20.00

    2.   Black dutch shoe, mark, "McCOY." $20.00 - $25.00

    3.   Blue flower, no mark. Made in 1946.
                    Price per pair - $32.00 - $45.00

ROW 2:

    1.   Pink flower, no mark. Made in 1946. $15.00 - $20.00

    2.   Blue dutch shoe, mark, "McCOY." Made in 1947. $20.00 - $25.00

    3.   Tan flower, no mark. Made in 1946. $15.00 - $20.00

ROW 3:

    1.   Flower, green with some brown trim, no mark. $15.00 - $20.00
           Made in 1946.

    2.   Yellow dutch shoe, mark, "McCOY." Made in 1947. $20.00 - $25.00

    3.   Flower, green with lots of brown trim, no mark, $15.00 - $20.00
           Made in 1946.

Miscellaneous

This chapter is made up of wall pockets that we do not have enough of for a chapter of their own, or that we can not identify. We have done our best to identify as many as we could, but with so many with no markings, it's impossible to identify them all.

ROW 1:
1.   Peacock, trimmed with gold, no mark. $15.00 - $20.00

2.   Peacock, brown, no mark. $15.00 - $20.00

3.   Peacock, trimmed with gold, no mark.
      (Same as number 1 but opposite)
                                 Price per pair - $35.00 - $45.00

ROW 2:
1.   Boy on sliding board, trimmed with gold, no mark. $15.00 - $25.00

2.   Bird and flower, trimmed with gold, no mark. $35.00 - $45.00

3.   Angel playing mouth harp, mark incised "8307." $15.00 - $25.00

ROW 3:
1.   Lady and horn of plenty, mark, in black letters, $30.00 - $40.00
      "JAN. 52."

2.   Lady and rose, mark incised, "8662-L." $40.00 - $50.00

Miscellaneous

ROW 1:

   1.   Blue cherub, no mark. $7.00 - $9.00

   2.   Blue vase, shape, no mark. Same type of finish $7.00 - $9.00
and color. Bought together and should be sold as
a set.   Price per pair - $15.00 - $20.00

ROW 2:

   1.   Boy with mandolin, trimmed with gold, mark, $35.00 - $45.00
incised, "C-N."

   2.   Violin and musical note, no mark. $25.00 - $30.00

ROW 3:

   1.   Banjo, trimmed with gold, mark, incised, $25.00 - $30.00
"© MOYER."

   2.   Violin and hand, trimmed with gold, no mark. $20.00 - $35.00

   3.   Violin, trimmed with gold, mark, incised, $25.00 - $30.00
"© MOYER." Made in 1940's thru 1950's.

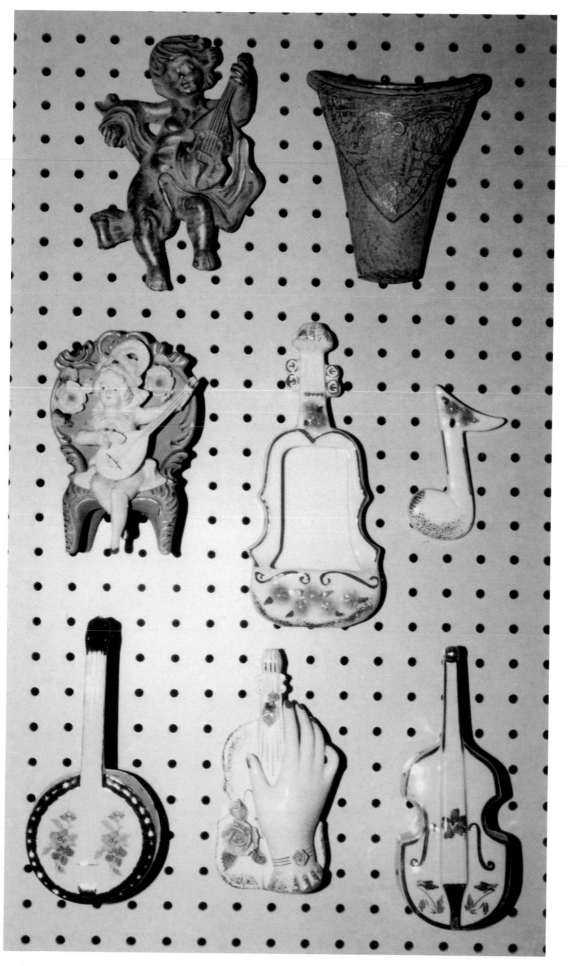

Miscellaneous

ROW 1:
1. Pansies on book with "THE LORD'S PRAYER," trimmed with gold, no mark. $7.00 - $12.00

2. Book with "TO MOTHER," and trimmed with gold, no mark. $7.00 - $12.00

3. Pansies on scroll with "TWENTY-THIRD PSALM," and trimmed with gold, no mark. $7.00 - $12.00

ROW 2:
1. Madonna, no mark. $15.00 - $20.00

2. Mary, trimmed with gold, no mark. $15.00 - $20.00

3. Madonna, no mark. $15.00 - $20.00

ROW 3:
1. Pink roses, trimmed with gold, no mark. $10.00 - $15.00

2. Baby and swan, trimmed with gold. $15.00 - $20.00

3. Mary, trimmed with gold, no mark. $15.00 - $20.00

ROW 4:
1. Bird, aqua color, mark, in blue letters, "© THE LOVE BIRDS - THE LOVE OF THESE LITTLE BIRDS WILL SYMBOLIZE THIS HOME, AN EXPRESSION WITHOUT WORDS, FOR BY THEIR PRESENCE THIS IS KNOWN." $10.00 - $15.00

2. Hand and fan, trimmed with gold, no mark. $20.00 - $25.00

3. Bird, yellow color, mark in blue letters "© THE LOVE BIRDS - THE LOVE OF THESE LITTLE BIRDS WILL SYMBOLIZE THIS HOME, AN EXPRESSION WITHOUT WORDS, FOR BY THEIR PRESENCE THIS IS KNOWN." $10.00 - $15.00

Price per pair - $22.00 - $32.00

162

Miscellaneous

ROW 1:

1. Pink roses and blue bows, no mark. $7.00 - $10.00

2. Aqua color, no mark. $15.00 - $20.00

3. White with pink top, no mark. $10.00 - $12.00

ROW 2:

1. Aqua color, no mark. $10.00 - $12.00

2. Pink flower, no mark. $20.00 - $25.00

3. Aqua color, no mark.   Price per pair - $22.00 - $25.00

ROW 3:

1. Pink flower, trimmed with gold, no mark. $15.00 - $20.00

2. White with vertical lines, no mark. $10.00 - $15.00

3. White with fancy scroll design, no mark. $20.00 - $25.00

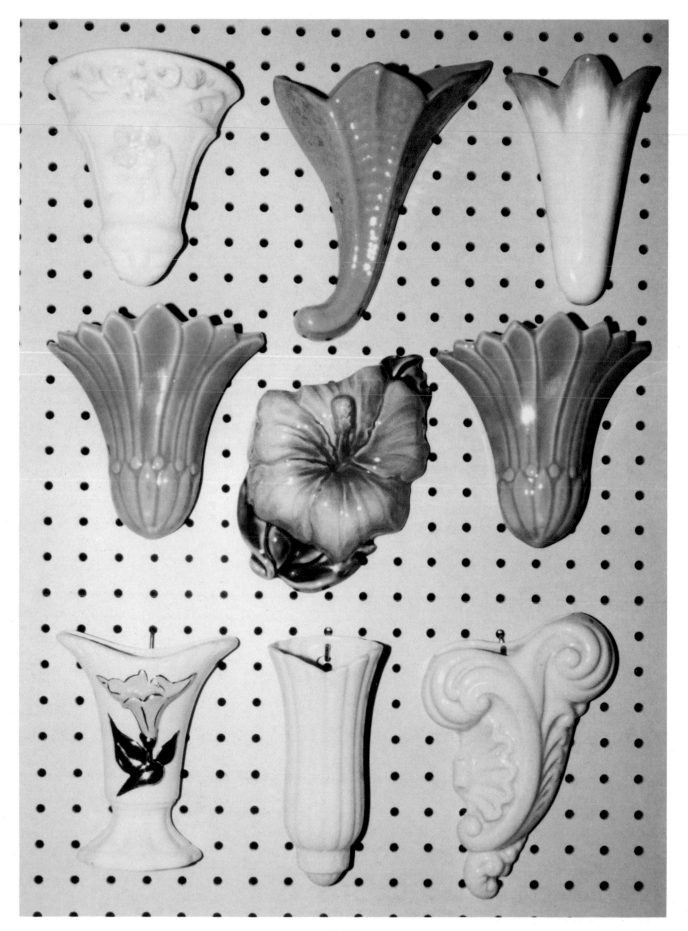

164

Miscellaneous

ROW 1:

1. Multi-color flowers, trimmed with gold, no mark. $10.00 - $15.00

2. Dutch woman, trimmed with gold, mark, incised, "4078." $20.00 - $25.00

3. Multi-color flowers, trimmed with gold, no mark.
   Price per pair - $25.00 - $35.00

ROW 2:

1. Violin, trimmed with gold, no mark. $15.00 - $20.00

2. Girl and flowers, trimmed with gold, no mark. $15.00 - $20.00

3. Violin, trimmed with gold, no mark.
   Price per pair - $35.00 - $45.00

ROW 3:

1. Lady with dark hair, trimmed with gold, no mark. $20.00 - $25.00

2. Lady with blond hair, trimmed with gold, no mark.
   Look like Gibson girls.   Price per pair - $45.00 - $55.00

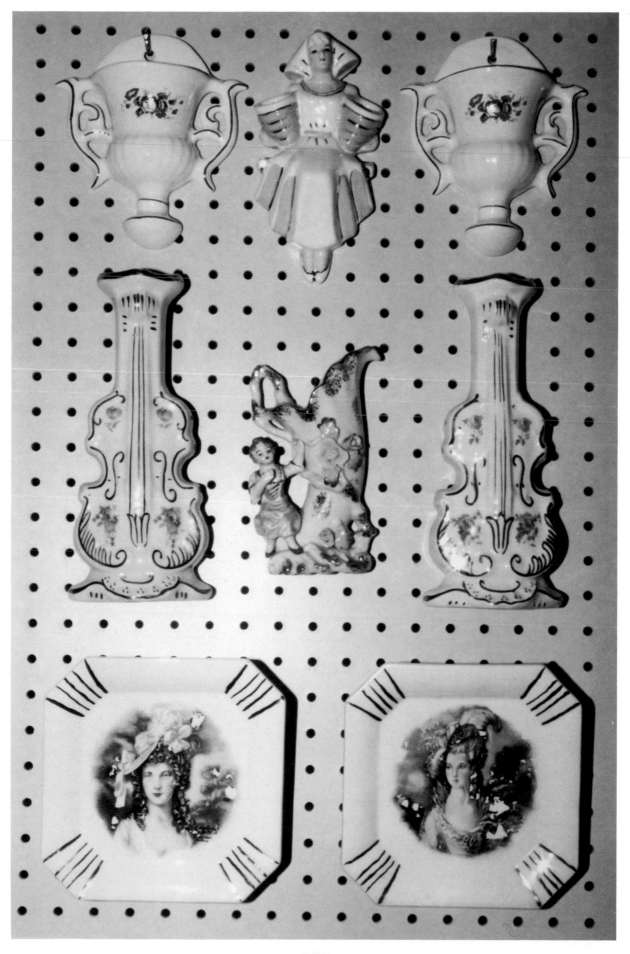

Miscellaneous

ROW 1:

1. Blue violin, trimmed with gold, no mark. $15.00 - $20.00

2. White violin, trimmed with gold, mark, in gold letters, "WARRANTED 22K GOLD." $15.00 - $20.00

3. Blue violin, trimmed with gold, no mark.
   Price per pair- $35.00 - $45.00

ROW 2:

1. Mauve violin, no gold, no mark. $10.00 - $15.00

2. Blue violin, lighter in color, trimmed with gold, mark, in gold letters, "GOLDRA E. PALESTINE. O." $15.00 - $20.00

3. Mauve violin, trimmed with gold, no mark. Original price on bottom is 69 cents. $15.00 - $20.00

ROW 3:

1. Dark blue violin, trimmed with gold, mark, in gold letters, "GOLDRA E. PALESTINE O." $15.00 - $20.00

2. Tan violin, trimmed with gold, no mark. $15.00 - $20.00

3. Dark blue violin, trimmed with gold, mark, in gold letters, "GOLDRA E. PALESTINE O."
   Price per pair - $35.00 - $45.00

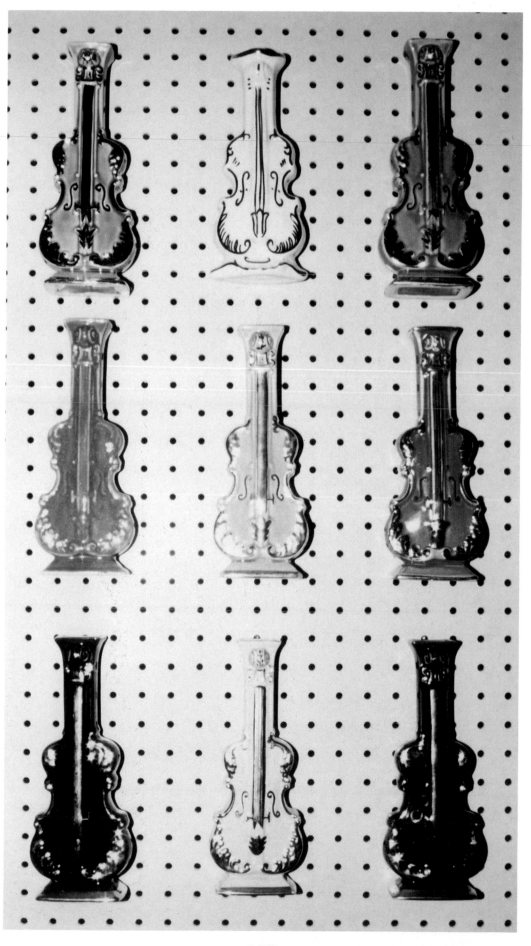

Miscellaneous

ROW 1:

    1.   White with brown cattail plants, no mark. $10.00 - $15.00

    2.   Longest one we have, 16" long, no mark, but $30.00 - $40.00
made by the Rocky Mountain Pottery of Loveland,
Colorado. We have only found two in our travels,
but are sure there are many more out there.

    3.   White with brown dry flowers, no mark, $10.00 - $15.00
This one and #1.   Price per pair - $25.00 - $35.00

ROW 2:

    1.   White with blue flowers, no mark. $10.00 - $15.00

    2.   White with pine cones and needles, mark, "ROMCO $15.00 - $20.00
USA." Made by Rocky Mountain Pottery of Loveland,
Colorado, early 1950's thru 1960's.

    3.   White with blue flowers, no mark.
                             Price per pair - $25.00 - $35.00

170

Miscellaneous

ROW 1:

1.   Kissing Dutch girl, no mark. $15.00 - $20.00

2.   Black cat woman, trimmed with gold, no mark. $25.00 - $30.00

3.   Kissing Dutch boy, no mark, goes with Dutch girl $15.00 - $20.00
   as a pair.

                          Price per pair - $35.00 - $45.00

ROW 2:

1.   Oriental lady with "COMEDY MASK," no mark. $15.00 - $20.00

2.   Brown, mark, incised, "STANDFORD-SEBRING. $20.00 - $25.00
   O. 267-E USA."

3.   Oriental man with "TRAGEDY MASK," no mark. $15.00 - $20.00

               #1 and #3 priced per pair - $35.00 - $45.00

ROW 3:

1.   Blue fan, trimmed with gold, mark, in gold letters, $10.00 - $15.00
   "MILFORD POTTERY BY KLAYKRAFT." This one is
   shown with side view.

2.   Plate with cherries, mark, incised, "STANFORD- $20.00 - $25.00
   SEBRING. O. 299."

3.   Blue fan, trimmed with gold, mark, in gold letters, $10.00 - $15.00
   "MILFORD POTTERY BY KLAYKRAFT." This one is
   shown with end view.   Price per pair - $25.00 - $35.00

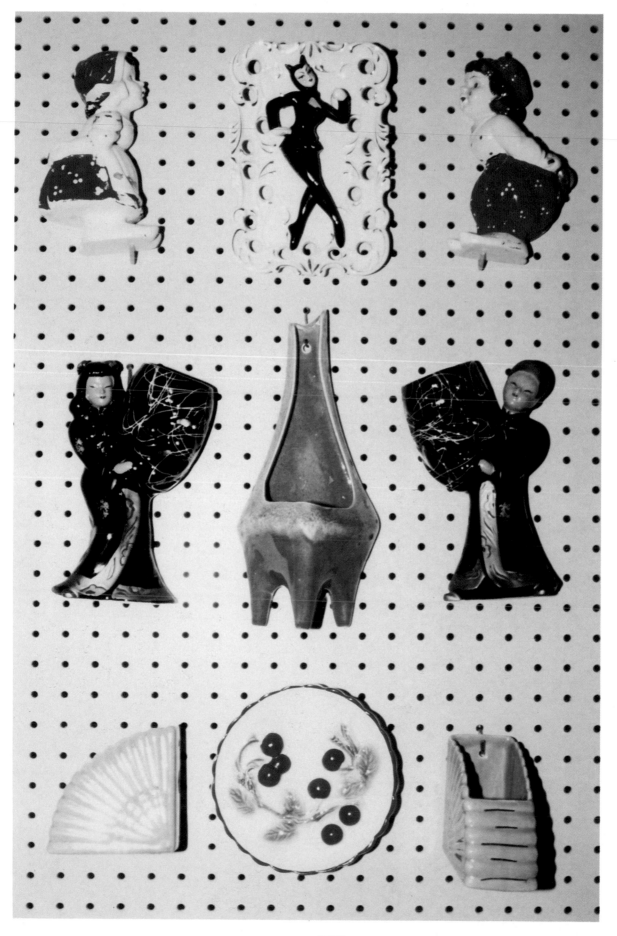

Miscellaneous

ROW 1:
    1.   Butterfly, mauve color, no mark. $7.00 - $10.00

    2.   Butterfly, gray and pink color, no mark. $7.00 - $10.00

ROW 2:
    1.   Large green butterfly, no mark. $25.00 - $30.00

    2.   Small green butterfly, no mark. $5.00 - $10.00

ROW 3:
    1.   Small pink butterfly, trimmed with gold, no mark. $7.00 - $10.00

    2.   Large pink butterfly, trimmed with gold, no mark. $15.00 - $20.00
                                   Price per pair - $25.00 - $35.00

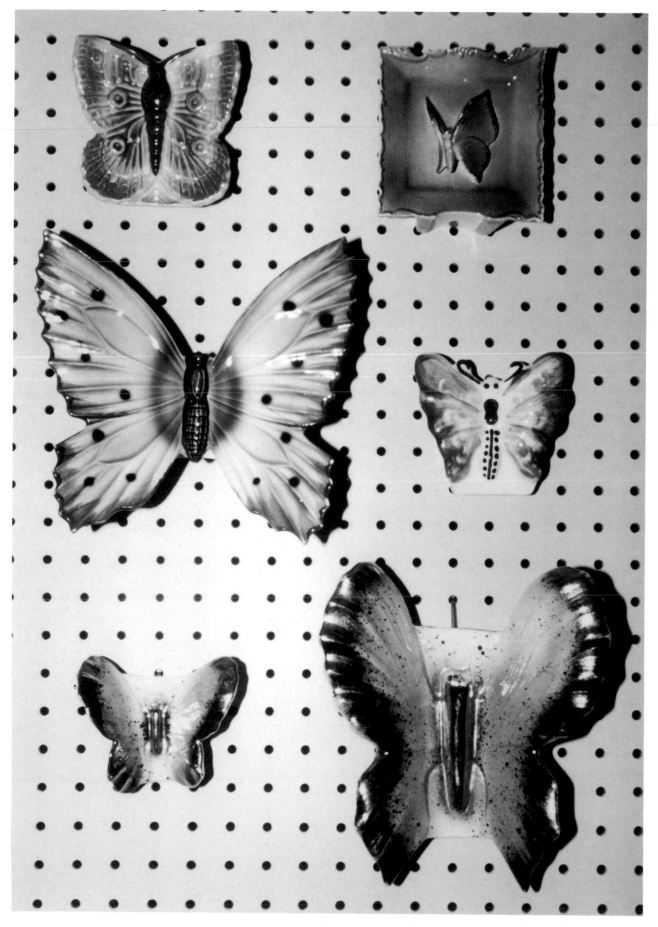

174

Miscellaneous

ROW 1:

   1.   Flying eagle, mark, in black letters, "©HOLT 1950." $15.00 - $20.00

   2.   Flying brown bird, no mark. $25.00 - $30.00

   3.   Flying eagle, mark, in black letters, "©HOLT 1950."   Price per pair - $35.00 - $45.00

ROW 2:

   1.   Large pink flying bird, no mark. $25.00 - $30.00

   2.   Stork, no mark. $6.00 - $10.00

ROW 3:

   1.   Bird at nest, mark, incised, "902," and in red letters, "EAST." $20.00 - $25.00

   2.   Large aqua color flying bird, no mark. $25.00 - $30.00

ROW 4:

   Red head parrot, no mark. $25.00 - $30.00

Miscellaneous

ROW 1:
    1.   Black fan, no mark. $7.00 - $10.00

    2.   Bamboo, no mark. $10.00 - $12.00

    3.   Black fan, no mark.   Price per pair - $15.00 - $21.00

ROW 2:
    1 and 2 are white with gold trim, each-no mark. $15.00 - $20.00
                                                      Price per pair - $35.00 - $45.00

ROW 3:
    1.   Yellow with red and blue flowers, no mark. $15.00 - $20.00
        Original price on back 50 cents.

    2.   Black with gold trim, no mark. $15.00 - $20.00

    3.   Yellow with red rose, no mark. $10.00 - $15.00

178

Miscellaneous

ROW 1:

1. Skillet trimmed with green and has strawberry pattern, no mark. $15.00 - $20.00

2. Dust pan, strawberry pattern, no mark. $20.00 - $25.00

3. Skillet trimmed with pink and has strawberry pattern, no mark. $15.00 - $20.00

ROW 2:

1. Cup, handle on left side. Strawberry pattern, no mark. $15.00 - $20.00

2. Iron, strawberry pattern, no mark. $15.00 - $20.00

3. Cup, handle on right side, strawberry pattern, no mark. This cup is different from #1 cup. Original price on back 89 cents. $15.00 - $20.00

ROW 3:

1. Teapot, strawberry pattern, no mark. $20.00 - $25.00

2. Dust pan, strawberry pattern, no mark. $10.00 - $15.00

3. Scoop, ivy pattern, no mark. $10.00 - $15.00

ROW 4:

Rolling pin, ivy pattern, no mark. $10.00 - $15.00

ROW 5:

Pitcher, strawberry pattern, no mark. $20.00 - $25.00

Miscellaneous

ROW 1:

    1.   Apple, yellow with red ripe spot, no mark. $15.00 - $20.00

    2.   Apple, red with light green leaves, no mark. $15.00 - $20.00

    3.   Apple, yellow, no mark. $15.00 - $20.00

ROW 2:

    1.   Apple, red with light green leaves, no mark. $15.00 - $20.00

    2.   Apple, red, no mark. $15.00 - $20.00

    3.   Apple, red with dark green leaves, no mark. $15.00 - $20.00

ROW 3:

    1.   Apple, red with leaves pointed down, no mark. $15.00 - $20.00

    2.   Apple, red, no mark. $15.00 - $20.00

    3.   Apple, red with leaves pointed up, no mark. $15.00 - $20.00

182

Miscellaneous

ROW 1:
1.   Pear, no mark. $15.00 - $20.00

2.   Bananas, no mark. $15.00 - $20.00

3.   Pear with ripe red spot, no mark. $15.00 - $20.00

ROW 2:
1.   Small strawberry, no mark. $15.00 - $20.00

2.   Bananas with leaves, no mark. $15.00 - $20.00

3.   Large strawberry, no mark. $15.00 - $20.00

ROW 3:
1.   Pear, no mark. $15.00 - $20.00

2.   Red apple, no mark. $15.00 - $20.00

3.   Lemon, no mark. $15.00 - $20.00

The fruit in row 3 are a set. Price per set of three $50.00 - $62.00

Miscellaneous

ROW 1:
1.   Grapes, pink, no mark.   \$15.00 - \$20.00

2.   Strawberries and leaves, no mark.   \$10.00 - \$15.00

3.   Grapes, green, no mark.   \$15.00 - \$20.00

ROW 2:
1.   Grapes, large bunch of purple color, no mark.   \$15.00 - \$20.00

2.   Lemon and leaves, no mark.   \$15.00 - \$20.00

3.   Grapes, small bunch of purple color, mark, in blue   \$10.00 - \$15.00
   letters, "50574."

ROW 3:
1.   Strawberry, no mark.   \$7.00 - \$10.00

2.   Cherries, no mark.   \$10.00 - \$12.00

ROW 4:
1.   Brown and yellow planter, incised, "FLOWER   \$10.00 - \$15.00
   HOUSE."

2.   Pink planter, incised, "FLOWER HOUSE."   \$10.00 - \$15.00

186

Miscellaneous

ROW 1:

1. Dutch shoe, small yellow, mark, in pencil on bottom, "OCT-1948." $7.00 - $10.00

2. Dutch shoe, pink rose, no mark. $5.00 - $7.00

3. Dutch shoe, yellow daisy, no mark. $5.00 - $7.00

4. Dutch shoe, blue windmill, mark, in blue letters, "ELESVA (CROWN) HOLLAND 015." $7.00 - $10.00

ROW 2:

1. Dutch shoe, blue floral, mark, in blue letters, "XXXDP DEIFT." $10.00 - $15.00

2. Dutch shoe, pink roses, trimmed with gold, no mark. $25.00 - $30.00

3. Dutch Shoe, cream, no mark. $7.00 - $10.00

4. Dutch shoe, blue floral, mark, in blue letters, "HAND PAINTED DEIFTS BLAUW, " and with paper label, "HOLLAND FLORAL INC. MADE IN TAIWAN, PATENTED SC-3." $10.00 - $12.00

ROW 3:

1. Dutch shoe, blue windmill, mark, in black letters, "4 © GEERLINGS GRHS. INC., MADE IN CHINA." $10.00 - $12.00

2. Dutch shoe, multi-color flowers, trimmed with gold, mark, in gold letters, "(CROWN) H.B. GUPREGNON BELGIUM." $25.00 - $30.00

3. Dutch shoe, gold, no mark. $30.00 - $35.00

4. Dutch shoe, blue windmill, mark, in blue letters, "104 DEIFTS HOLLAND HANDGESCNILDERD DMXWE." $15.00 - $20.00

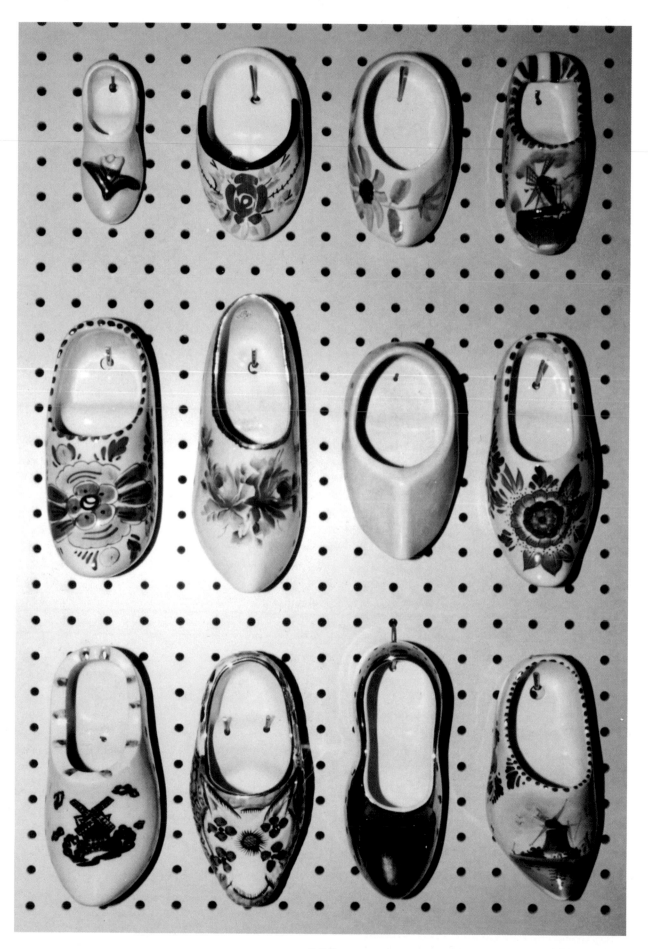

Miscellaneous

ROW 1:

1. Shoe, purple grapes, trimmed with gold, mark, in gold letters, "MC, JAN. 64." $25.00 - $30.00

2. Baby shoe, pink, no mark. $5.00 - $7.00

3. Shoe, red poinsettia flower, mark, in red letters, "HAND PAINTED, THE XMAS CITY NOEL, MO." $20.00 - $25.00

4. Baby Shoe, pink lace, no mark. $5.00 - $7.00

5. Shoe, green grapes, trimmed with gold, mark, in gold letters, "MC 64." $25.00 - $30.00

ROW 2:

1. Pair of black cowboy boots, no mark.
   Price per boot - $3.00 - $5.00
   Price per pair - $7.00 - $12.00

2. Red XMAS stocking, no mark. $15.00 - $20.00

3. Pair of pink cowboy boots, no mark.
   Price per boot - $3.00 - $5.00
   Price per pair - $7.00 - $12.00

ROW 3:

1. Cowboy boot, aqua color, no mark. $3.00 - $5.00

2. Boot, green, no mark. $5.00 - $10.00

3. Boot, dark brown, no mark. $5.00 - $10.00

4. Boot, aqua color, no mark. $5.00 - $10.00

5. Cowboy boot, white, no mark. $3.00 - $5.00

Miscellaneous

ROW 1:

1. Horse head, no mark. $10.00 - $15.00

2. Iron with pink flower, no mark. $5.00 - $7.00

3. Horse head, no mark.   Price per pair - $22.00 - $32.00

ROW 2:

1. Tiny black iron, no mark. $5.00 - $7.00

2. Gun, black, mark, incised, "PAT - PND." $20.00 - $25.00

3. Holster, white, mark on front, "*KEYSTONE," and on back side in green letters, "DILLON." $25.00 - $30.00

ROW 3:

1. Iron, yellow with green handle, no mark. $10.00 - $12.00

2. Iron, black, no mark. $10.00 - $12.00

3. Iron, mauve, no mark. $12.00 - $15.00

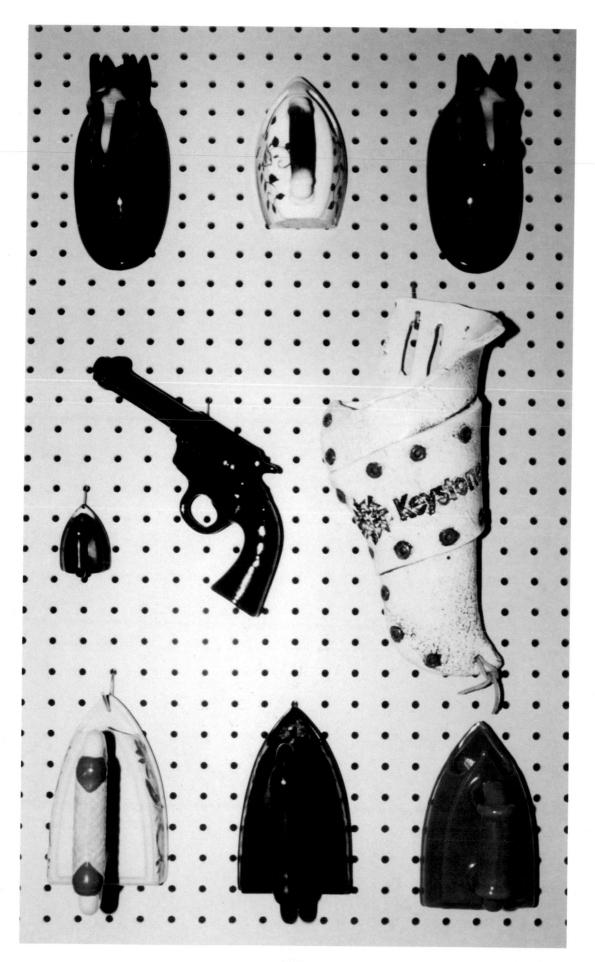

Miscellaneous

ROW 1:

    1.   Cat in pink bag, no mark. $12.00 - $15.00

    2.   Blue bib overalls, no mark. $10.00 - $15.00

    3.   Cat in brown bucket, no mark. $15.00 - $20.00

ROW 2:

    1.   Green horse shoe with black horse. $20.00 - $25.00

    2.   Back side of #1, "FOUR LEAF CLOVER" and
"GOOD LUCK."   Price per pair - $45.00 - $55.00

    3.   Green horse shoe with green horse head, no mark. $20.00 - $25.00

ROW 3:

    1.   Kissing Dutch girl in blue, no mark, this is half of
a pair. $10.00 - $15.00

    2.   Blue horse shoe with blue horse head, no mark. $20.00 - $25.00

    3.   Rocking horse, pink, no mark. $15.00 - $20.00

Miscellaneous

ROW 1:
    1.   Elf and yellow leaves, no mark. $8.00 - $12.00

    2.   Dumbo and mouse, mark, incised, "DUMBO © $40.00 - $50.00
WALT DISNEY PROD."

    3.   Elf and blue flowers, no mark. $8.00 - $12.00

ROW 2:
    1.   Deer head, mark, in black letters, "PY-NC." $25.00 - $30.00

    2.   Elf and green leaves, no mark. $8.00 - $12.00

    3.   Deer standing, no mark. $10.00 - $12.00

ROW 3:
    1.   Deer, yellow, no mark. $8.00 - $10.00

    2.   Gazelle, on pink, no mark. $20.00 - $25.00

    3.   Deer, grown, no mark.   Price per pair - $17.00 - $21.00

ROW 4:
    1.   Chipmunk, no mark. $8.00 - $10.00

    2.   Two black dogs, no mark. $15.00 - $20.00

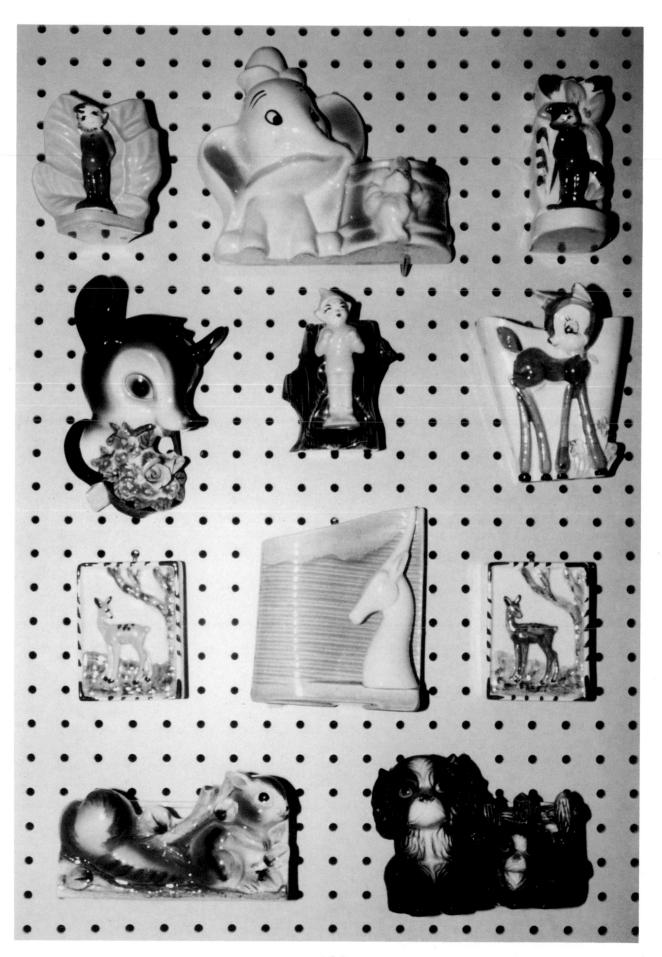

Miscellaneous

ROW 1:

    1.   Bird house, chartreuse, no mark. $8.00 - $10.00

    2.   Bird house, brown, no mark. $8.00 - $10.00

    3.   Bird house, yellow, no mark. $8.00 - $10.00

ROW 2:

    1.   Green bird on yellow, no mark. $8.00 - $10.00

    2.   Dog with pups, no mark. $25.00 - $30.00

    3.   Green bird on brown color, no mark. $8.00 - $10.00

ROW 3:

    1.   Bird house, blue, no mark. $15.00 - $20.00

    2.   Three owls, no mark, this can also be found to be used as a planter with no hole in the back. $10.00 - $15.00

    3.   Bird house, aqua color, no mark. $15.00 - $20.00

ROW 4:

    1.   Yellow birds and flowers, mark, in gold letters, "XXX-? DECORATING CO. BELOIT, OHIO." $15.00 - $20.00

    2.   Wishing well, gray, no mark. $15.00 - $20.00

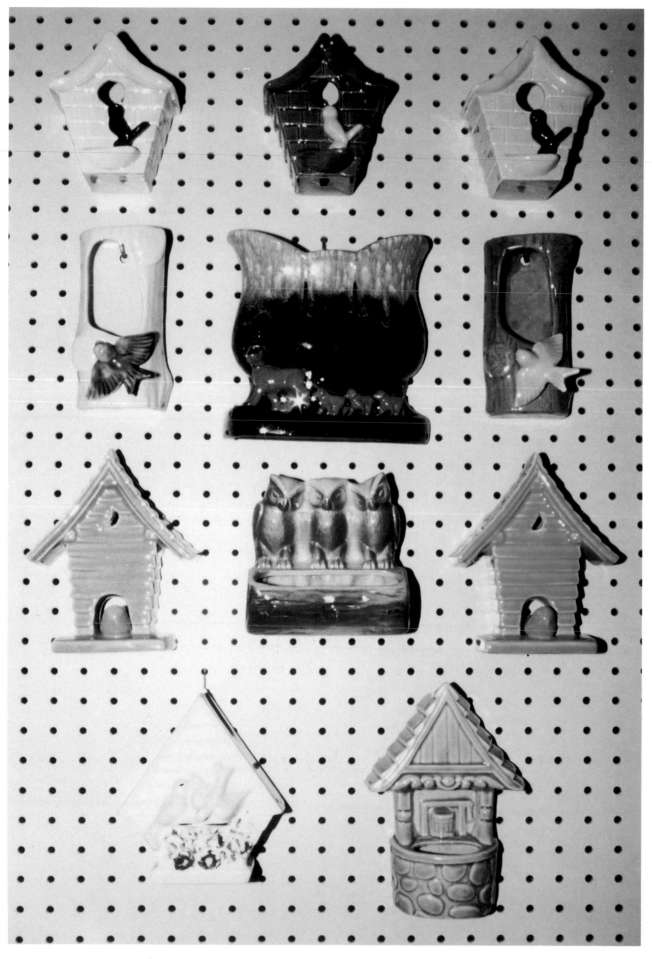

Miscellaneous

ROW 1:
    1.   Blue bird on plate, no mark. $25.00 - $30.00

ROW 2:
    1.   Parakeets, yellow and aqua, no mark. $12.00 - $15.00

    2.   Duck, blue and yellow, trimmed with gold, $15.00 - $25.00
            no mark.

    3.   Parakeets, yellow and mauve, no mark. $12.00 - $15.00

    All four wall pockets with parakeets in row 2,
    #1 and #3, and row 3, #1 and #3,, are all of the
    same pattern, but are all in different colors.

ROW 3:
    1.   Parakeets, yellow and brown, no mark. $12.00 - $15.00

    2.   Duck, black, gray and mauve, trimmed with $15.00 - $25.00
            gold, no mark.

    3.   Parakeets, yellow and blue, no mark. $12.00 - $15.00

ROW 4:
    1.   Yellow duck on mauve color. $12.00 - $20.00

    2.   Mauve duck on blue color. $12.00 - $20.00

ROW 5:
    1.   Mauve duck on green color. $12.00 - $20.00

    2.   Yellow duck on pink color. $12.00 - $20.00

    All wall pockets in rows 4 and 5, are marked,
    "PATENTED 149144."

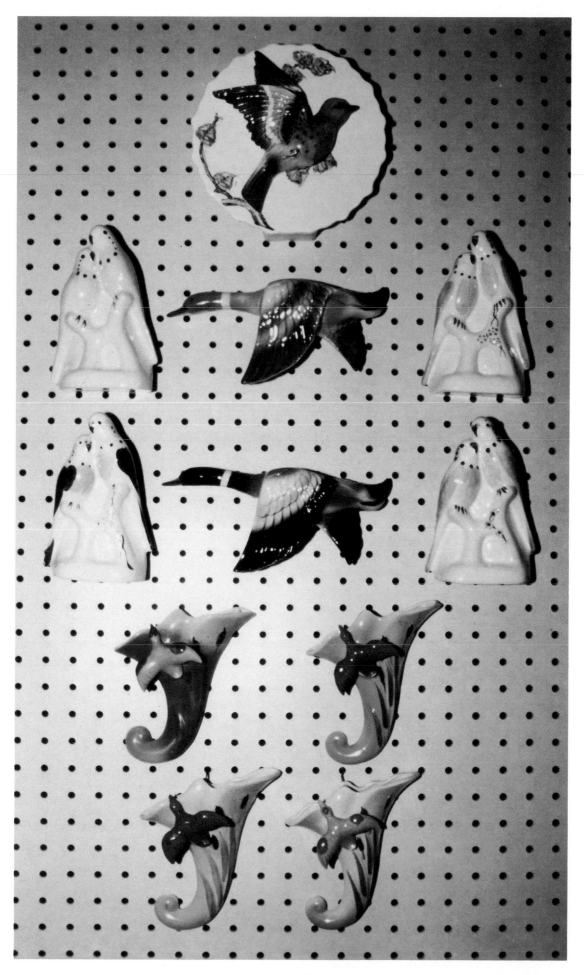

Miscellaneous

ROW 1:

    1.   Dark bird on limb, no mark. $15.00 - $20.00

    2.   Black bird at hole in tree, mark, incised, "10156." $10.00 - $15.00

    3.   Bird with yellow beak on limb, no mark. $15.00 - $20.00

ROW 2:

    1.   Parakeets, blue with yellow heads, no mark. $15.00 - $20.00

    2.   Parakeets, green, trimmed with gold, no mark. $15.00 - $25.00

    3.   Parakeets, one yellow and one mauve, trimmed with gold, no mark. $15.00 - $25.00

ROW 3:

    1.   Bird and leaves, ivory color, no mark. $15.00 - $20.00

    2.   Bird and leaves, blue color, no mark. $15.00 - $20.00

    3.   Bird and leaves, tan color, no mark. $15.00 - $20.00

ROW 4:

    1.   Colorful owl, no mark. $15.00 - $20.00

    2.   Butterfly and leaves, no mark. Made on same pattern as the wall pockets in row #3. $15.00 - $20.00

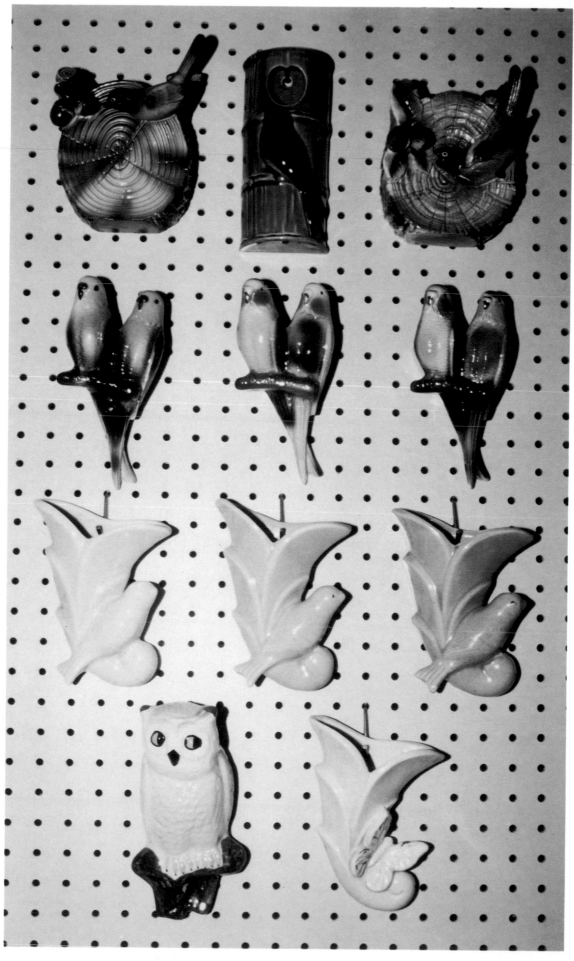

Miscellaneous

ROW 1:
1.   Pink wishing well, no mark. $8.00 - $10.00

2.   Yellow floral design, no mark. $15.00 - $20.00

3.   Pink wishing well, no mark.   Price per pair - $17.00 - $21.00

ROW 2:
1.   Green wishing well, trimmed with gold, mark, in $12.00 - $15.00
gold, letter, "A."

2.   Mauve leaf, mark, blue paper label with silver $20.00 - $25.00
letters, "AUTHENTIC FENTON HAND MADE."

Somewhere I have read, or during my many miles
of travel, I picked up this information.   The Fenton
Glass company, during the mid years of their
manufacturing, experimented into a line of pottery.
Could this be one? If so, is it a rare and valuable item?

3.   Green wishing well, trimmed with gold, mark, in
gold, letter, "A."   Price per pair - $25.00 - $32.00

ROW 3:
1.   Mauve wishing well, no mark. Original price on $8.00 - $10.00
back 89 cents.

2.   Red rose and chartreuse leaves, no mark. $15.00 - $20.00

3.   Mauve wishing well, no mark. Price per pair - $17.00 - $21.00

ROW 4:
1.   Green wishing well, no mark. $8.00 - $10.00

2.   Brown flower, no mark. $10.00 - $15.00

3.   Green wishing well, no mark. $17.00 - $21.00

Miscellaneous

ROW 1:
1. Mexican man sleeping, no mark. $10.00 - $15.00

2. Wishing well, no mark. $15.00 - $20.00

3. Blue bird, no mark. $10.00 - $15.00

ROW 2:
1. Pink rose, no mark. $10.00 - $15.00

2. Wishing well, no mark. $15.00 - $20.00

3. Red rose, no mark. $10.00 - $15.00

ROW 3:
1. Purple flowers on blue, no mark. $10.00 - $15.00

2. Purple flowers on green, no mark. $10.00 - $15.00

3. Purple flowers on yellow, no mark. $10.00 - $15.00

ROW 4:
1. Light green with scroll design, mark, incised, "2". $15.00 - $20.00

2. Blue pot, no mark. $15.00 - $20.00

Miscellaneous

ROW 1:

1. Horn of plenty, clear glass, no mark. $20.00 - $30.00

2. Horn of plenty, looks like Frankoma, no mark. $20.00 - $30.00

3. Horn of plenty, clear glass, no mark.
                     Price per pair - $45.00 - $65.00

ROW 2:

1. Glass, mauve, with two bubbles, no mark. $10.00 - $15.00

2. Small glass, pink and mauve, with two bubbles, $10.00 - $12.00
trimmed with gold, mark, in red letters, "COPYRIGHT
© CERAMICRAFT, SAN CLEMENTE, CALIF."

3. Glass with two bubbles, no mark. $10.00 - $125.00

                     Price per pair - $22.00 - $32.00

ROW 3:

1. Green with darker green bottom, no mark. $5.00 - $7.00

2. Horn of plenty, dark gray, mark, incised, "73 US." $20.00 - $30.00

3. Green with lighter colored rim, mark, in black $5.00 - $7.00
letters, "TAMAC PERRY, OKLA. USA.

208

Miscellaneous

ROW 1:

     Large gray rooster, no mark. $20.00 - $25.00

ROW 2:

1.   Hen, mark, incised, "916 MADE IN US." $25.00 - $35.00

2.   Rooster, mark, incised, "915 MADE IN US." $25.00 - $30.00

Both the hen and rooster stand in metal baskets for hangers.   Price per pair - $55.00 - $75.00

ROW 3:

1.   Rooster, mauve, mark, incised, "3." $10.00 - $15.00

2.   Rooster, green, mark, incised, "4." $10.00 - $15.00

3.   Rooster, blue, mark, incised, "1." $10.00 - $15.00

All three roosters are of same pattern, but in different colors.

NOTE:

It's strange, but we find more Roosters than Hens. We are sure that they were made in pairs because we have some. Most we have bought separately and paired up later. We don't know why the hens are more scarce, but since they are, they bring a premium price.

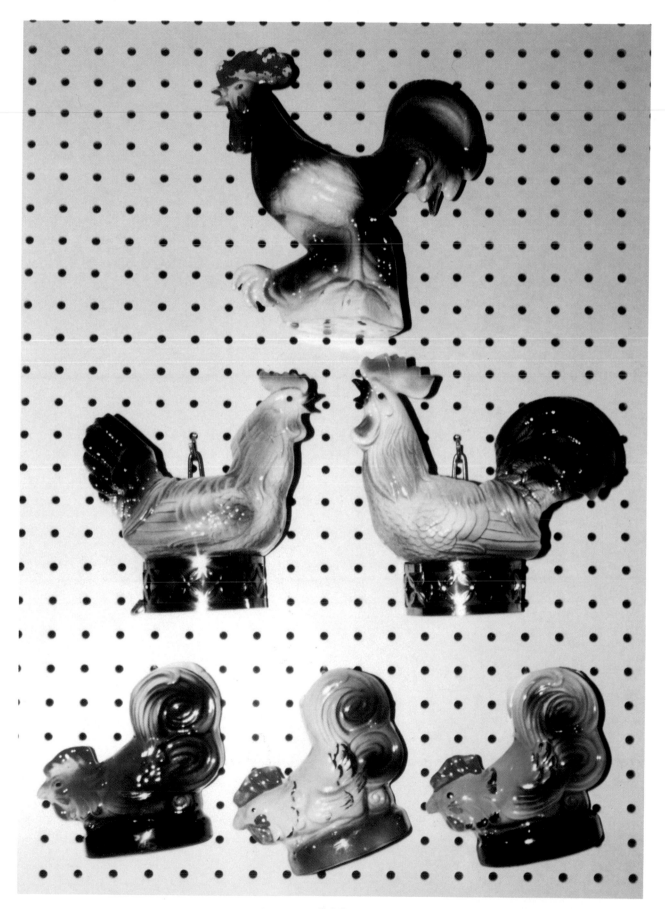

Miscellaneous

ROW 1:

    1.   Blue rooster on plate, no mark. $20.00 - $25.00

    2.   Colorful rooster, no mark. $15.00 - $20.00

ROW 2:

    1.   Hen, yellow and green with closed eyes, no mark. $10.00 - $15.00

    2.   Rooster, yellow and green with open eyes. Original $10.00 - $15.00
        price on back 79 cents.

                                  Price per pair - $25.00 - $35.00

ROW 3:

    1.   Rooster, plain gray, no mark. $15.00 - $20.00

    2.   Rooster same as above, but had painted accent $15.00 - $20.00
        on it.

Miscellaneous

ROW 1:

    1.   Teapot clock. 5 'til 2 o'clock, no mark. $10.00 - $12.00

    2.   Large white pigeon, no mark. $20.00 - $25.00

    3.   Clock, 8 'til 12 o'clock, no mark. $10.00 - $12.00

ROW 2:

    1.   Owl clock, 10 after 10 o'clock, two pendulums, no mark. $10.00 - $15.00

    2.   Large cuckoo clock, 3 o'clock, three pendulums, no mark. $35.00 - $45.00

    3.   Owl clock, 10 after 10 o'clock, two pendulums, no mark.   Price per pair - $22.00 - $32.00

ROW 3:

    1.   Cuckoo clock with blue bird, 22 after 7 o'clock, no mark. $10.00 - $12.00

    2.   Grandfather clock, 20 'til 2 o'clock. Also has a real thermometer on the front at 72 degrees, no mark. $15.00 - $20.00

    3.   Clock, orange color, trimmed with gold, 20 after 2 o'clock, no mark. $10.00 - $12.00

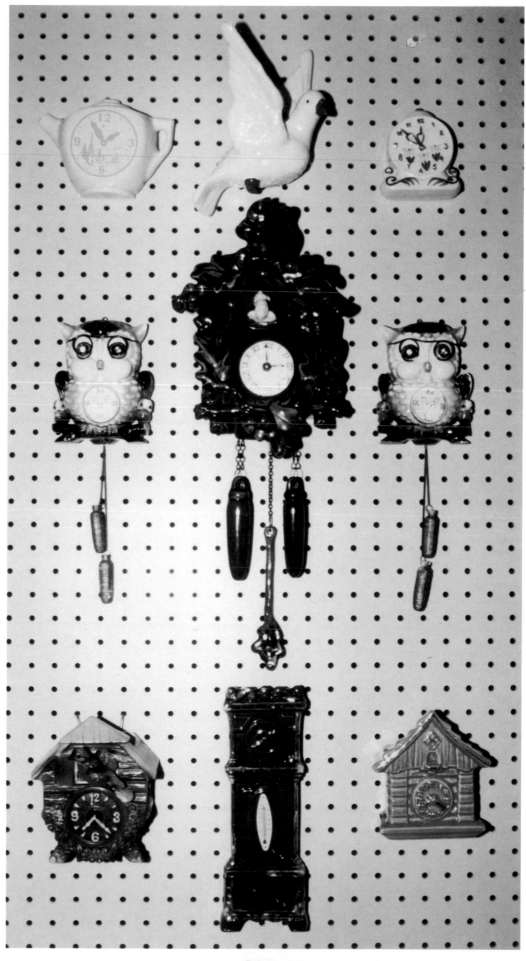

214

Miscellaneous

ROW 1:

    Bird house with blue bird on a long wire spring, no mark. $20.00 - $25.00

ROW 2:

1. Brown cuckoo clock, 3 o'clock, trimmed with gold, two pendulums, no mark. $20.00 - $25.00

2. Large cuckoo clock, 3 o'clock, three pendulums, no mark. $25.00 - $35.00

3. Green cuckoo clock, 15 'til 12 o'clock, trimmed with gold, two pendulums, no mark. $20.00 - $25.00

ROW 3:

1. Yellow clock, 3 after 5 o'clock, no mark. $15.00 - $20.00

2. Blue clock, 4 o'clock, no mark. $10.00 - $15.00

3. Clock with Dutch windmill, 22 after 8 o'clock, no mark. $20.00 - $25.00

216

Miscellaneous

ROW 1:

    1.   Clock, white with mauve color. $10.00 - $15.00

    2.   Cuckoo clock, 3 o'clock, three pendulums, no mark. $25.00 - $35.00

    3.   Clock, white, 8 'til 2 o'clock, no mark. $7.00 - $10.00

ROW 2:

    1.   Cuckoo clock, light blue, 4 o'clock. The two pendulums are of the same color as the clock, and they are tied on with cord. No mark. $20.00 - $30.00

    2.   Cuckoo clock, green, 4 o'clock, two pendulums, no mark. $20.00 - $30.00

    The above two clocks are made on the same pattern, but are of different colors, and have different types of pendulums.

ROW 3:

    Cuckoo clock, 3 o'clock, sits in a metal holder and has two metal pendulums, mark, incised, "313 US." $25.00 - $35.00

Miscellaneous

ROW 1:
1. Fish, brown, pink and green colors, trimmed with gold, mark, incised, "3." $15.00 - $20.00

2. Large fish, pink and black, no mark. $20.00 - $25.00

ROW 2:
1. Sea shell, mother of pearl color, trimmed with gold, no mark. $15.00 - $20.00

2. Happy gray fish, no mark. $15.00 - $20.00

3. Sea shell, black and pink, no mark. $10.00 - $15.00

ROW 3:
1. Yellow fish, no mark. $15.00 - $20.00

2. Sea shell, no mark. $15.00 - $20.00

3. Black fish, no mark. $15.00 - $20.00

ROW 4:
1. Happy fish, black and yellow and has gold paint trim, no mark. $15.00 - $20.00

2. Sea shell, no mark. $15.00 - $20.00

3. Sea horse, no mark. $15.00 - $20.00

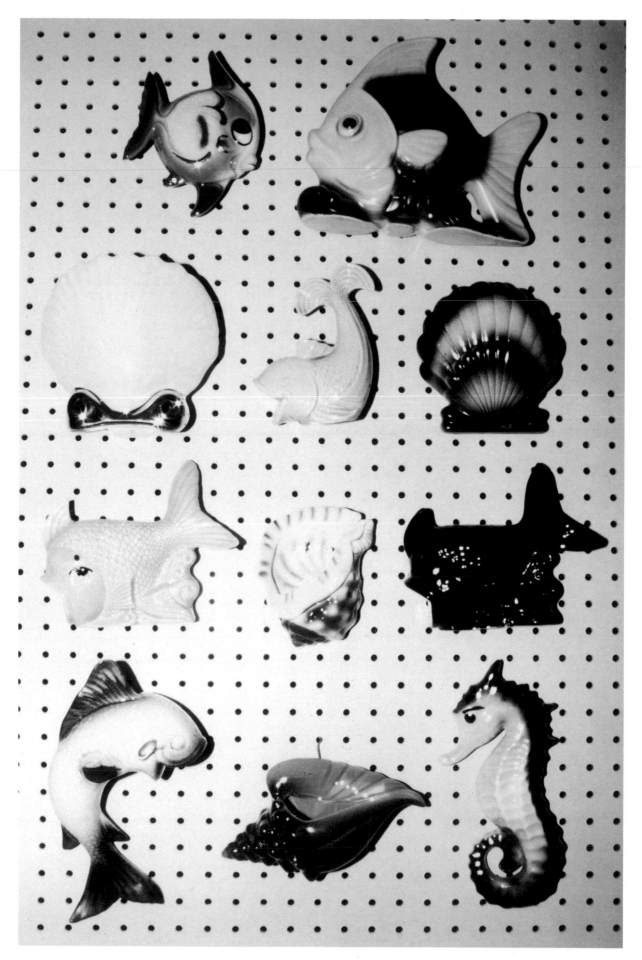

Miscellaneous

ROW 1:
1. White lily, mark, incised, "377," and in blue letters, "ABINGDON." $40.00 - $60.00

2. Green flower pots, mark, incised, "640," and in blue letters, "ABINGDON, U.S.A." $30.00 - $40.00

ROW 2:
1. Mauve flowers, no mark. $10.00 - $15.00

2. Yellow flowers, no mark. $10.00 - $15.00

3. Mauve flowers, no mark.   Price per pair - $22.00 - $32.00

ROW 3:
1. Mauve flower, no mark. $15.00 - $20.00

2. Yellow with green leaves, mark, incised, "PATENT-PENDING," and in black letters "5596 A COVENTRY MADE IN USA." $15.00 - $20.00

3. Aqua blue flower, no mark. Made on same pattern as #1. $15.00 - $20.00

ROW 4:
White deco design, trimmed with gold, no mark. $15.00 - $20.00

222

Miscellaneous

ROW 1:

   1.   Pink dogwood flower, no mark. $20.00 - $25.00

   2.   Bamboo with leaves, no mark. $15.00 - $20.00

   3.   Multi-color brown leaf, mark, incised, "JAMIESON CERAMICS©." $7.00 - $12.00

ROW 2:

   1.   Green leaves, no mark. $10.00 - $12.00

   2.   Large leaf, no mark. $25.00 - $30.00

   3.   Yellow leaves, no mark. $15.00 - $20.00

ROW 3:

   1.   Multi-color green leaf, mark, incised, "JAMIESON CERAMICS ©." $10.00 - $15.00

   2.   Large leaf, no mark. $25.00 - $30.00
       Same as large leaf in row 2, #2.
                            Price per pair - $55.00 - $65.00

   3.   Multi-color brown, yellow and green leaf, mark, incised, "JAMIESON CERAMICS ©." $10.00 - $15.00

ROW 4:

   1.   Green leaves, trimmed with gold, no mark. $15.00 - $20.00

   2.   Multi-color brown, mark, in gold numbers, "73." $15.00 - $20.00

   3.   Green with pine cones, trimmed with gold, no mark. $15.00 - $20.00

Miscellaneous

ROW 1:

    1.   Flower, white, yellow center, trimmed with brown, no mark. $8.00 - $10.00

    2.   Flower, green with pink center, no mark. $10.00 - $12.00

    3.   Flower, white, yellow center, trimmed with brown, no mark.   Price per pair - $17.00 - $22.00

ROW 2:

    1.   Flower, green, no mark. $5.00 - $7.00

    2.   Large yellow sunflower, no mark. $10.00 - $12.00

    3.   Flower, white, no mark. $5.00 - $7.00

ROW 3:

    1.   Flower, yellow with pink center, no mark. Original price on back 29 cents. $15.00 - $20.00

    2.   Flower, green, no mark. $10.00 - $12.00

    3.   Flower, yellow, no mark. Original price on back 59 cents. $10.00 - $12.00

ROW 4:

    1.   Blue flower, no mark. $8.00 - $10.00

    2.   Flower, mauve with green leaves, no mark. $15.00 - $20.00

    3.   Flower, mauve, no mark. $15.00 - $20.00

226

Miscellaneous

ROW 1:

1. Hat, white with mauve trim and brown bow, no mark. $10.00 - $12.00

2. Large yellow hat, no mark. $10.00 - $15.00

3. Hat, brown with mauve flower, no mark. $12.00 - $15.00

ROW 2:

1. Small green hat, no mark. $5.00 - $7.00

2. Large green hat, no mark. $10.00 - $10.00

3. Small green hat, no mark.   Price per pair - $12.00 - $15.00

         Price per set of three - $25.00 - $30.00

ROW 3:

1. Hat with blue bow and flowers, mark, paper label, "FAMILY BUSINESS CERAMICS, MIKE & PEGGY CONYERS 1516 5TH STREET BOON, IA. 50036." $10.00 - $15.00

2. Large hat, chartreuse, no mark. $15.00 - $20.00

3. Hat, pink with roses, trimmed with gold, no mark. $20.00 - $25.00

Miscellaneous

ROW 1:

    1.   Hat, multi-color flowers with red bow, no mark. $20.00 - $25.00

    2.   Large green hat, no mark. $10.00 - $15.00

    3.   Hat, pink with blue bow and red cherries, kitten looking over brim, no mark. $15.00 - $20.00

ROW 2:

    1.   Hat, green with pink center, gold painted bow, no mark. $15.00 - $20.00

    2.   Black hat, no mark. $10.00 - $15.00

    3.   Hat, aqua blue, no mark. Same pattern as #1. $15.00 - $20.00

ROW 3:

    1.   Balloon, blue and white, no mark. $15.00 - $20.00

    2.   Umbrella, white and pink, no mark. $30.00 - $40.00

Miscellaneous

ROW 1:
  1.   Maroon color with elf, no mark. $15.00 - $25.00

  2.   Water well, green with elf, no mark. $15.00 - $20.00

ROW 2:
  1.   Oriental woman carrying baskets, no mark. $10.00 - $12.00

  2.   Oriental woman carrying lanterns, no mark. $10.00 - $12.00

  3.   Oriental man carrying baskets, no mark. $10.00 - $12.00

         #1 woman and #3 man price per pair - $20.00 - $25.00

ROW 3:
  1.   Green color with elf, no mark. $15.00 - $25.00

  2.   Elf by well with spider web in background, no $20.00 - $25.00
       mark.

ROW 4:
  1.   Mauve leaves, no mark. $10.00 - $15.00

  2.   Maroon color with deer, no mark. $15.00 - $25.00

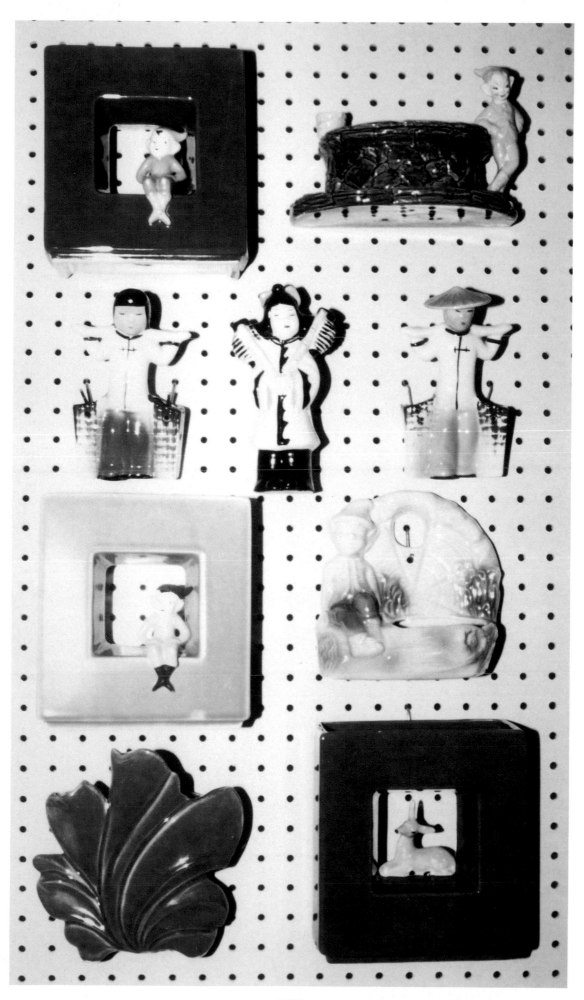

Miscellaneous

ROW 1:

1. Small white, multi-color flowers, trimmed with gold, mark, in black letters, "PORCELANA SCHMIDT RIDDOTESTO S. CATARINA." $15.00 - $20.00

2. Small heart, trimmed with copper, on front "KELHEIM," mark, incised, "637." $15.00 - $20.00

ROW 2:

1. Lamp, aqua color, trimmed with gold, no mark. $15.00 - $20.00

2. Hanging lamp, brown and yellow, no mark. $15.00 - $20.00

3. Lamp, pink, trimmed with gold, no mark. $15.00 - $20.00

ROW 3:

1. White with mauve leaves, no mark. $10.00 - $12.00

2. Lamp, green and pink, no mark. $15.00 - $20.00

3. Lamp, pink, trimmed with gold, no mark. $15.00 - $20.00

ROW 4:

1. Mouse hanging in a yellow shirt, mark, incised, "© CASTLE." $20.00 - $25.00

2. Lamp, white with brown trim, no mark. $15.00 - $20.00

Miscellaneous

ROW 1:

1. Corner wall pocket, multi-color fruit design, has mark in blue, but can't read it. $20.00 - $30.00

2. White with blue dragon design, no mark. $20.00 - $25.00

3. Corner wall pocket, aqua color, mark, in black letters, "HANDMADE." $30.00 - $35.00

ROW 2:

1. Blue with vertical lines, no mark. $15.00 - $20.00

2. Green, art deco design, no mark. $30.00 - $40.00

3. Brown, no mark. $15.00 - $20.00

ROW 3:

1. Small white head, no mark. $10.00 - $15.00

2. Oriental boy on plate, no mark. $20.00 - $25.00

3. Little Oriental girl, mauve color, no mark. $15.00 - $20.00

236

Miscellaneous

ROW 1:

1. Blue, trimmed with gold, mark, incised, "F&F DRIFTWOOD CERAMICS- MIAMI, FLA." $8.00 - $12.00

2. Telephone, trimmed with brown, no mark. $12.00 - $15.00

3. Blue and black, no mark. $5.00 - $7.00

ROW 2:

1. Brown telephone, no mark. $7.00 - $12.00

2. Basket, no mark. $15.00 - $20.00

3. Green telephone, no mark. $10.00 - $15.00

ROW 3:

1. Salt box, speckled black and white color with cherries, no mark. $8.00 - $10.00

2. Basket, yellow and brown color, no mark. $15.00 - $20.00

3. Dust pan, speckled black and white color with one cherry, no mark. $6.00 - $10.00

ROW 4:

1. Green mailbox, no mark. $10.00 - $15.00

2. White deco design, no mark, have found this one as a planter with no hole in back. $8.00 - $12.00

Miscellaneous

ROW 1:

1. Apron, plaid design, mark, in black letters, $15.00 - $20.00
"RELIABLE GLASSWARE POTTERY, 1956-508 B."

2. Pitcher and bowl, blue, mark, "E 4491 (World) $15.00 - $20.00
INARCO ®."

ROW 2:

1. Yellow toilet, marked on front, "HILLBILLY FOOT $10.00 - $12.00
BATH." No mark on back.

2. Spinning wheel, marked on front, "BUSY HANDS $25.00 - $30.00
MAKE A HAPPY HEART!" Incised on back,
"HAND PAINTED©."

3. White with green flowers. $6.00 - $12.00

ROW 3:

1. Green bellows, mark, in black letters, "E 3576 $10.00 - $12.00
(WORLD) INARCO ®."

2. Brown square with scene of grandfather clock $10.00 - $15.00
and umbrellas in stand, no mark.

3. Brown bellows, mark, incised, "WOODLAND." $10.00 - $15.00

Miscellaneous

ROW 1:

1.	Large fork, no mark.	$5.00 - $10.00
2.	White with green plate, trimmed with gold, no mark.	$20.00 - $30.00
3.	Large spoon, no mark.	$5.00 - $10.00
	Fork and spoon price per pair -	$12.00 - $22.00

ROW 2:

1.	Cup and saucer, pink no mark.	$12.00 - $15.00
2.	Cup and saucer, white with green trim, no mark, crockery, very old.	$20.00 - $25.00
3.	Cup and saucer, green, no mark.	$12.00 - $15.00

ROW 3:

1.	Pitcher and bowl, white, trimmed with blue, no mark. Original price on back $1.00.	$10.00 - $15.00
2.	Large cup with plaid design, no mark.	$12.00 - $15.00
3.	Pitcher and bowl, white and chartreuse, no mark.	$10.00 - $15.00

242

Miscellaneous

ROW 1:
1. Cup and saucer, purple, trimmed with gold, mark, in gold letters which we can't read. $25.00 - $30.00

2. Cup and saucer, green, mark, incised, "SENEGAL CHINA." $12.00 - $15.00

3. Cup and saucer, white, trimmed with gold, mark, incised, "N.S. Co. Clev. O. U.S.A. S.P. 3." $20.00 - $25.00

ROW 2:
1. Cup and, saucer, white, trimmed with mauve, no mark. $15.00 - $20.00

2. Cup and saucer, mauve and chartreuse, no mark. $10.00 - $15.00

3. Cup and saucer, white with pink roses, no mark. $20.00 - $25.00

ROW 3:
1. Cup and saucer, trimmed with blue, has purple plums, mark, incised, "N.S. Co. Clev. O. U.S.A. S.P.3." $15.00 - $20.00

2. Cup and saucer, pink, no mark. $10.00 - $12.00

3. Cup and saucer, white, trimmed with yellow and has colorful fruit, mark, incised, "N.S. Co. Clev. O. U.S.A. S.P.3." $15.00 - $20.00

ROW 4:
1. Cup, green and white with blue bird, no mark. Handle on left. $8.00 - $10.00

2. Cook stove, white, trimmed with gold, no mark. $20.00 - $25.00

3. Cup, green and white with blue bird, no mark. Handle on right. $8.00 - $10.00

           Price per pair - $18.00 - $22.00

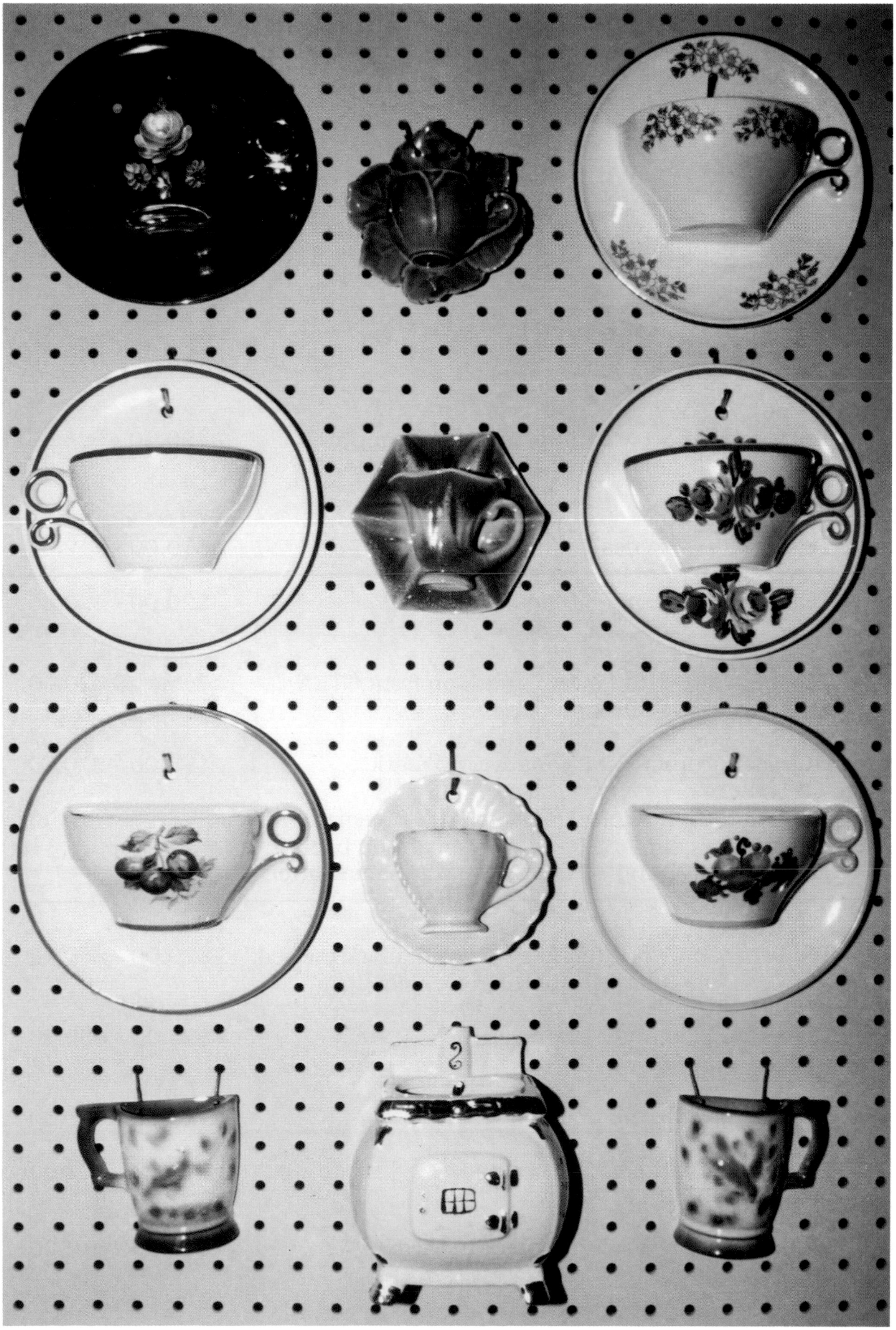

Morton's Potteries

Morton's Potteries were in business in Morton, Illinois for 99 years; 1877 through 1976. The first pottery was started by six brothers, named Rapp, from Burgberg, Germany, making brick and tile. They went on to make mixing bowls and other utility items, and in later years, art pottery. The names of the potteries were changed several times over the years, but the Rapp family was always involved with the pottery business in Morton, Illinois. The wall pockets we show in this chapter were made by Midwest Pottery Inc., and Morton Pottery Company. Since so many of their products were not marked, other potteries get credit for a lot of their wall pockets.

Thanks to Doris and Burdell Hall who wrote a book, MORTON'S POTTERIES: 99 YEARS, we have been able to identify the wall pockets we show here, along with the catalog numbers which we have included in our description.

ROW 1:
1.   Multi-color lattice and pot, #467, no mark. $20.00 - $25.00

2.   Lady watering flowers, #445, no mark. $20.00 - $30.00

3.   Multi-color lattice and pot, #467, no mark.
    Price per pair - $45.00 - $55.00

ROW 2:
1.   Lattice and pot with yellow flower, no mark. $15.00 - $20.00

2.   Lady watering flowers, #445, no mark. $20.00 - $30.00

3.   Lattice and pot with mauve color flower, no mark. $15.00 - $20.00

ROW 3:
1.   Green floral, no mark. $15.00 - $20.00

2.   Lattice and pot with blue flower, no mark. $15.00 - $20.00

3.   Brown floral, no mark. $15.00 - $20.00

All wall pockets on this page were made by Morton Pottery Company, 1922 through 1976.

Morton Potteries

ROW 1:

    1.   Pink hen, no mark. $30.00 - $35.00

    2.   White bird house with blue bird, #485, no mark. $10.00 - $12.00

    3.   Pink rooster, no mark. $25.00 - $30.00

                Hen and rooster price per pair - $60.00 - $75.00

ROW 2:

    1.   Black and white hen, no mark. $30.00 - $35.00

    2.   White bird house with red trim, and red bird, $10.00 - $12.00
            #485, no mark.

    3.   Rooster with majolica glaze, no mark. $25.00 - $30.00

ROW 3:

    1.   Love birds, #443, no mark. $10.00 - $15.00

    2.   Multi-color hen, no mark. $30.00 - $35.00

    3.   Love birds, made on same mold as #433, but the   RARE
            front was not cut out for use as a wall pocket.
            Instead, the back was cut out and a small hole
            was punched in the bottom for use as a stringer,
            No mark. RARE.

All wall pockets on this page were made by Morton Pottery Company, 1922 through 1976.

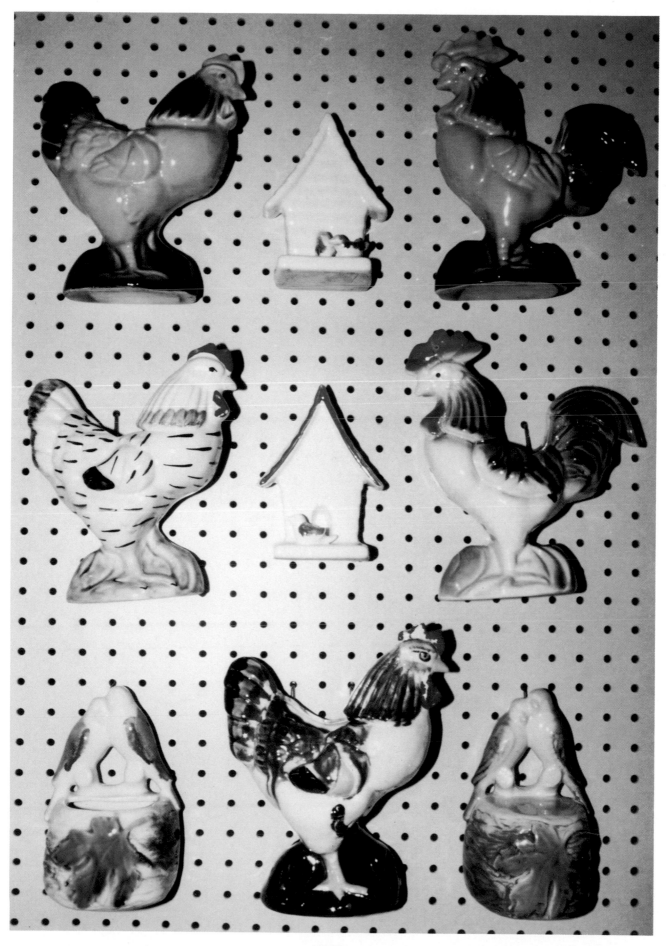

Morton Potteries

ROW 1:

1. Corner wall pocket, white with plums. This was made by Midwest Potteries, Inc., Morton, Illinois. It has been hand decorated with underglaze. This was an experimental item and never put on the production line. Very few of them were ever made. This happened in 1942 through 1943. — RARE

2. Green pig "SKEDOODLE", #672, mark, "PAT. PEND", also made as a bank. — $25.00 - $30.00

3. Parrot and grapes, no mark. — $25.00 - $30.00

ROW 2:

1. Blue peacock, #684, mark, "U. S. A." — $10.00 - $15.00

2. Cockateel, light color, #578, no mark. — $15.00 - $20.00

3. Pink peacock, #684, mark, "U.S.A." — $10.00 - $15.00

ROW 3:

1. Green peacock, #684, mark, "U.S.A." — $10.00 - $15.00

2. Cockteel, dark color, #578, no mark. — $17.00 - $22.00

3. White peacock, #684, mark, "U.S.A." — $10.00 - $15.00

The corner wall pocket #1 in row 1, was made by Midwest Potteries, Inc., 1940 through 1944. All the others on this page were made by Morton Pottery Company, 1922 through 1976.

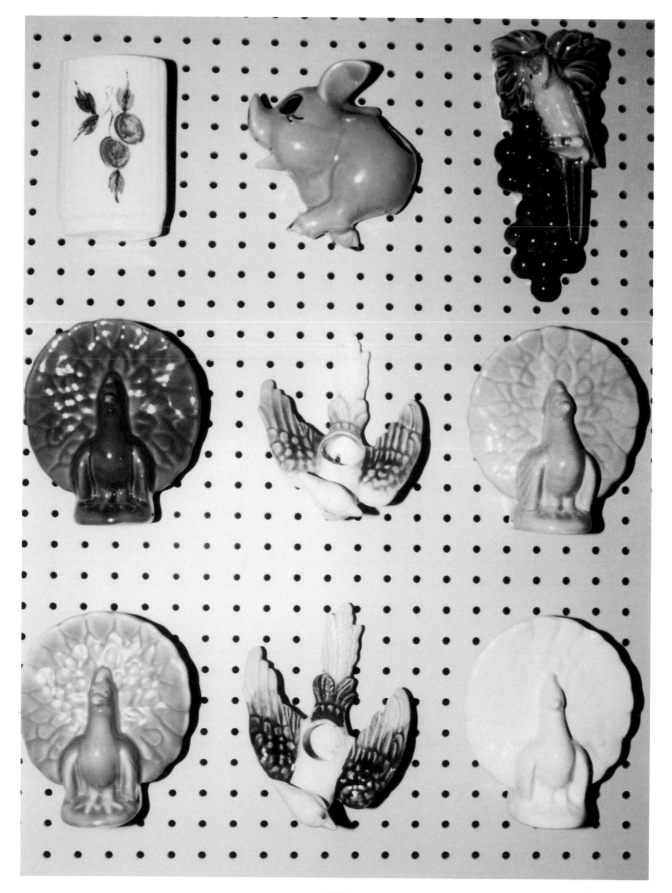

Morton Potteries

ROW 1:

1. Colorful bird with head down, #643, no mark. $15.00 - $20.00

2. Cockateel, large colorful bird, #424, no mark. $25.00 - $30.00

3. Colorful bird with head up, #700, no mark. $15.00 - $20.00

ROW 2:

1. White with blue flower, #644, no mark. $10.00 - $20.00

2. White with pink flower, #644 no mark. $10.00 - $20.00

3. White with yellow flower, #644, no mark. $10.00 - $20.00

ROW 3:

1. Owl on yellow quarter moon, no mark. Original price on bottom $1.50. $20.00 - $25.00

2. Pink with blue flower, #644, no mark. Original price on bottom 29 cents. $10.00 - $20.00

3. Owl on white quarter moon, no mark. $20.00 - $25.00

All the wall pockets in row 2 and #2 in row 3 are the same pattern, embossed diamond weave with flared floral spray, flared shape. Sold to stores for $2.24 per dozen.

Also, a majolica glaze was used on some of the Morton Potteries wall pockets.

All wall pockets on this page made by Morton Potteries Company, 1922 through 1976.

Red Wing Potteries

Red Wing Potteries Inc., operated 1936 through 1967 at Red Wing, Minnesota. This company started in 1878 as Red Wing Stoneware Company until 1906 becoming Red Wing Union Stoneware Company at that time. In 1936 it became Red Wing Potteries Inc., producing for the most part, crocks, jugs and flower pots, and some art pottery. Our five are the only wall pockets we have found, but we are sure there must have been others made.

ROW 1:
1. Cornucopia, pink, mark, "RED WING 441." $25.00 - $35.00

2. Violin, brown, mark, "RED WING U.S.A. 907." $20.00 - $30.00

3. Cornucopia, aqua color, mark, "RED WING 441." $25.00 - $35.00

ROW 2:
1. Violin, aqua color, mark, "RED WING USA $30.00 - $35.00
   M-1484," also red on gold paper label marked,
   "ART POTTERY."

2. Violin, black, mark, "RED WING USA M-1484," also $30.00 - $35.00
   red on gold paper label marked, "ART POTTERY."

Roseville

The Roseville Pottery Company, started in Roseville, Ohio in the early 1890's. During their years in business they made many beautiful wall pockets. Today they are the most sought after of all wall pockets and bring premium prices when you can find them.

Thanks to Jerry and Ann McClain of Higginsville, Missouri, for sharing their collection with us. Without them, we could not have had a chapter on Roseville.

ROW 1:
1.	Blackberry, 8 1/2", made in 1933, no mark.	$425.00 - $825.00
2.	Pine cone, brown, 8 1/2", made in 1931, mark, "Roseville."	$260.00 - $340.00
3.	Clematis, brown, 8 1/2" made in 1944, mark, "Roseville."	$150.00 - $200.00
4.	Clematis, blue, 8 1/2", made in 1944, mark, "Roseville."	$150.00 - $200.00

ROW 2:
1.	Apple Blossom, blue, 8 1/2", made in 1948, mark, "Roseville."	$125.00 - $175.00
2.	Apple Blossom, green, 8 1/2", made in 1948, mark, "Roseville."	$125.00 - $175.00
3.	Gardenia, blue, made in late 1940's, mark, "Roseville."	$145.00 - $200.00
4.	Gardenia, brown, made in late 1940's, mark, "Roseville."	$145.00 - $200.00

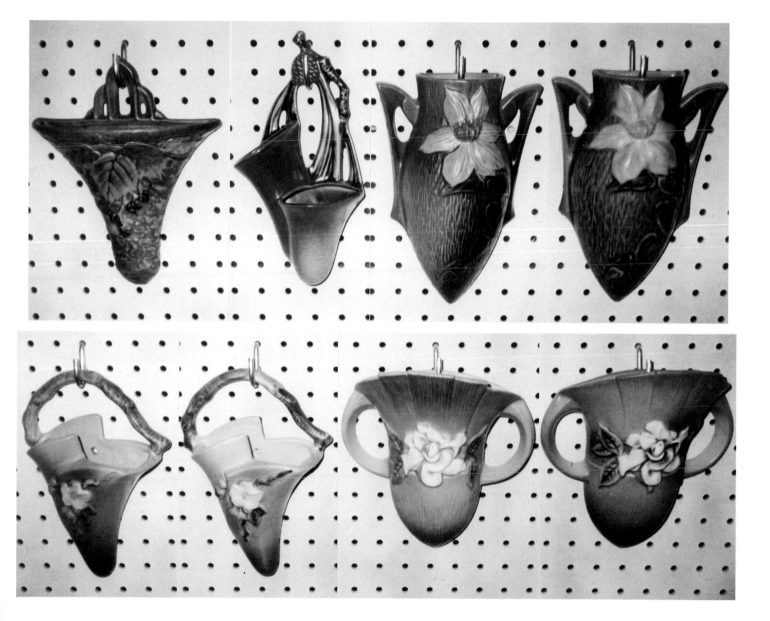

Roseville

ROW 1:

    1.   Donatello, 11 1/2", made in 1915, no mark. $150.00 - $200.00

    2.   Donatello, 9", made in 1915, no mark. $125.00 - $175.00

    3.   Carnelian I, blue, 8", made in 1910, mark, in letters, "RV." $125.00 - $175.00

    4.   Carnelian I, green, 8", made in 1910, mark, in letters, "RV." $125.00 - $175.00

ROW 2:

    1.   La Rose, 7 1/2", made in 1924, mark, in letters, "RV." $150.00 - $200.00

    2.   La Rose, 9", made in 1924, mark, in letters, "RV." $150.00 - $200.00

    3.   Freesia, 8 1/2", made in 1945, mark, "Roseville." $125.00 - $175.00

    4.   Foxglove, 8", made in 1942, mark, "Roseville." $250.00 - $300.00

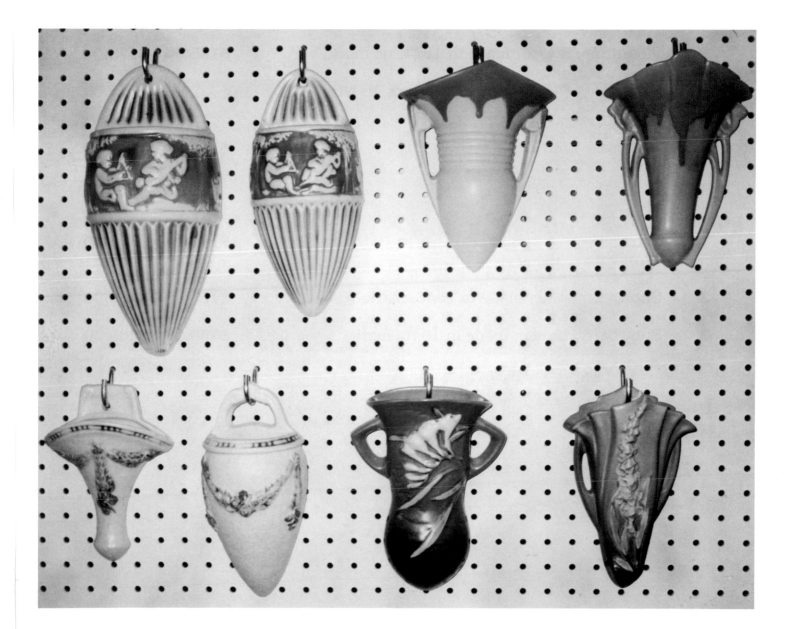

Roseville

ROW 1:

    1.   Wincraft, 8 1/2", made in 1948, mark, "Roseville." $125.00 - $175.00

    2.   Dahlrose, green, 9", made in 1924, no mark. $150.00 - $225.00

ROW 2:

    1.   Snowberry, green, made in 1946, mark, "Roseville." $150.00 - $200.00

    2.   Snowberry, dusty rose, made in 1946, mark, "Roseville." $150.00 - $200.00

ROW 3:

    1.   Ivory I, 10", made in 1916, no mark. $150.00 - $200.00

    2.   Mostique, 10 1/2", made in 1915, no mark. $150.00 - $200.00

Royal Copley
Head Wall Pockets

Royal Copley was produced by the Spaulding China Company in Sebring, Ohio from 1942 until 1957. It was sold to 5 and 10 cent stores. They made a very high quality pottery with beautiful colors and glazes, but for some reason they were not very collectable until recent years. They discontinued decorating with gold trim before 1948, but still made quality pottery. So many of Royal Copley's pieces had paper labels which, unless you know their style, makes it difficult to identify.

ROW 1:

1. Girl in green, mark, "ROYAL COPLEY." $20.00 - $25.00

2. Angel, blue, no mark, sold new with a paper label. $20.00 - $25.00

ROW 2:

1. Flower, blue, with bird, no mark. Identical to the $12.00 - $15.00
    Royal Copley ashtray mold.

2. Dog, brown, mark, "ROYAL COPLEY." $15.00 - $20.00

3. Bird, red, mark, "ROYAL COPLEY." $15.00 - $20.00

ROW 3:

1. Apple, red, mark, "ROYAL COPLEY." $15.00 - $20.00

2. Salt bowl, yellow, mark, "ROYAL COPLEY." Also $25.00 - $30.00
    paper label, gold on purple, marked, "ROYAL
    COPLEY."

3. Rooster, white, mark, "ROYAL COPLEY." $25.00 - $30.00

ROW 4:

Fruit plate, mark, "ROYAL COPLEY." $18.00 - $22.00

Royal Copley Head Wall Pockets

ROW 1:
1. Pirate, pink head band, mark, "ROYAL COPLEY." $35.00 - $40.00
    Also comes with gray head bands. Gray is most
    difficult to find.

2. Princess Blackamoor, with star on necklace. The $40.00 - $45.00
    Princess is the most difficult to find, marked, "ROYAL
    COPLEY."

ROW 2:
1. Prince Blackamoor, with plate on necklace, mark, $35.00 - $40.00
    "ROYAL COPLEY," also paper label, marked, "ROYAL
    COPLEY."

2. Prince Blackamoor, with plate on necklace, mark, $45.00 - $50.00
    "ROYAL COPLEY." This one has a white turban
    which is a rare color and difficult to find.

    Other pairs in other colors to look for:
    A. In gray and yellow,   Price per pair - $80.00 - $90.00

    B. In white, with white turban,
                                 Price per pair - $100.00 - $115.00

    C. Any color, trimmed with gold,
                                 Price per pair - $120.00 - $150.00

ROW 3:
1. Girl in gray, mark, " ROYAL COPLEY." $25.00 - $30.00

2. Girl in pink, mark, "ROYAL COPLEY 1." $25.00 - $30.00
    The above girls come in more colors. We have seen
    them in gray, pink, blue and dark mauve. The dark
    mauve is the most difficult to find. We would price
    the dark mauve at - $30.00 - $35.00

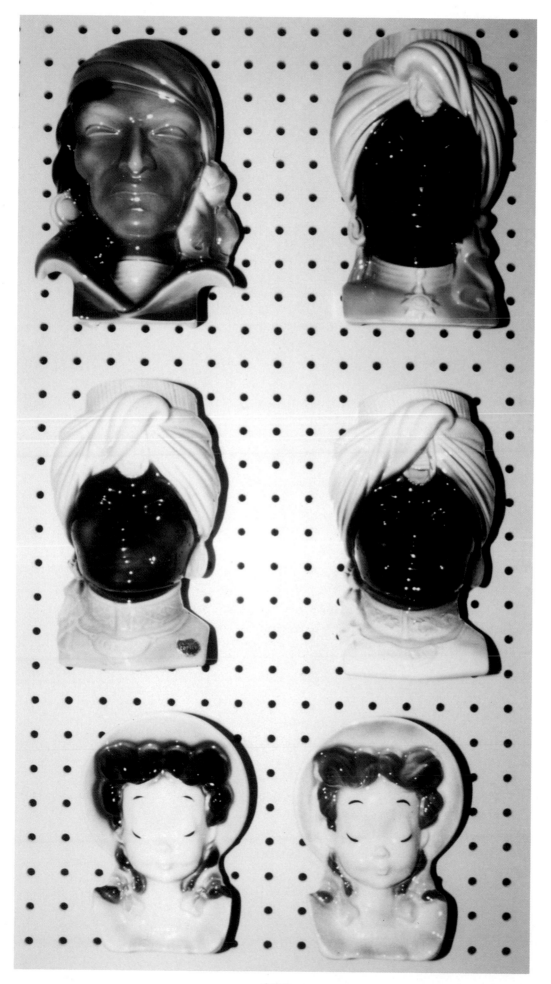

Royal Copley Head Wall Pockets

ROW 1:

1.   Chinese boy, lips puckered, green clothes, yellow hat, mark, "Royal Copley." $20.00 - $25.00

2.   Chinese boy, lips puckered, red clothes, gray hat, mark, "Royal Copley 3." $20.00 - $25.00

The above boys will always be found with puckered lips. Also, there were girls made with smiling lips. All can be found in the following colors:
> A. Green clothes with yellow hat.
> B. Green clothes with chartreuse hat.
> C. Red clothes with gray hat.
> D. Red clothes with blue hat.
> E. Red clothes with chartreuse hat.

NOTE: Ones with blue hats are difficult to find, but the chartreuse hats are very rare.

ROW 2:

1.   Colonial man, mark, "Royal Copley." $40.00 - $45.00

2.   Colonial woman, mark, "Royal Copley." $40.00 - $45.00

NOTE: The Colonial man is being reproduced in Japan, but is easy to spot because of lighter weight and color. Also, it is not marked with raised letters on back side.   **Price at -** $25.00 - $30.00

ROW 3:

1.   Boy, lips puckered, green clothes, rare chartreuse hat, mark, "Royal Copley." $25.00 - $30.00

2.   Girl, lips puckered, red clothes, blue hat, mark, "Royal Copley." $25.00 - $30.00

The above boy and girl can be found in the following colors:
> A. Green clothes with yellow hat.
> B. Green clothes with chartreuse hat.
> C. Red clothes with blue hat.

NOTE: Again, the chartreuse hats are rare.

Other Head
Wall Pockets

ROW 1:

    1.   Lady in pink, mark, "A." $25.00 - 430.00

    2.   Lady in yellow, mark, paper foil label, silver letters on silver background, "A NAPCO CREATION JAPAN." $30.00 - $35.00

ROW 2:

    1.   Lady in blue, trimmed with gold, mark, "U.S.A." $25.00 - $30.00

    2.   Lady in yellow, trimmed with gold, mark, "U.S.A." $25.00 - $30.00

    3.   Lady in mauve, trimmed with gold, mark, "U.S.A." $25.00 - $30.00

ROW 3:

    1.   Lady in yellow, no mark. $30.00 - $35.00

    2.   Girl in purple, no mark. $15.00 - $20.00

274

Other Head Wall Pockets

ROW 1:

1. Lady in pink, no mark. $30.00 - $35.00

2. Lady in green, no mark. $30.00 - $35.00

ROW 2:

1. Oriental boy with pigtail, no mark. $20.00 - $25.00

2. Oriental girl in green, no mark. $20.00 - $25.00

ROW 3:

1. Man, blond hair, no mark. $10.00 - $15.00

2. A native of India, dressed in black, trimmed with gold, no mark. $40.00 - $45.00

3. Man, brown hair, no mark. $10.00 - $15.00

276

Other Head Wall Pockets

ROW 1:

    1.   Little head, brown and white, no mark. $10.00 - $12.00

    2.   Oriental, black cap, no mark. $15.00 - $20.00

    3.   Little head, brown and white, no mark.

                               Price per pair - $22.00 - $27.00

ROW 2:

    1.   Oriental woman, blue and white porcelain, no mark. $20.00 - $25.00

    2.   Old man with long beard, no mark. $35.00 - $40.00

    3.   Oriental woman, blue and white procelain, no mark.   Price per pair - $45.00 - $55.00

ROW 3:

    1.   Lady with bonnet, no mark. $20.00 - $25.00

    2.   Lady with earrings, aqua color, trimmed with gold, no mark. $20.00 - $25.00

    3.   Lady in large hat, no mark. $35.00 - $45.00

Other Head Wall Pockets

ROW 1:

    Girl with plaid bow in hair, no mark. $15.00 - $25.00

ROW 2:

  1. Boy dressed in plaid, mark, incised, "SANDY D 230." $35.00 - $40.00

  2. Girl dressed in plaid, mark, incised, "JEAN 231." $35.00 - $40.00

                                 Price per pair - $75.00 - $85.00

ROW 3:

  1. Dutch boy, no mark. $12.00 - $15.00

  2. Dutch girl, no mark. $12.00 - $15.00

                                 Price per pair - $25.00 - $32.00

ROW 4:

  1. Old woman, mark, paper label, "HAND PAINTED MADE IN JAPAN." $20.00 - $22.00

  2. Cute little girl, mark, incised, "P 345." Also silver paper label, "NORCREST FINE CHINA JAPAN." $15.00 - $20.00

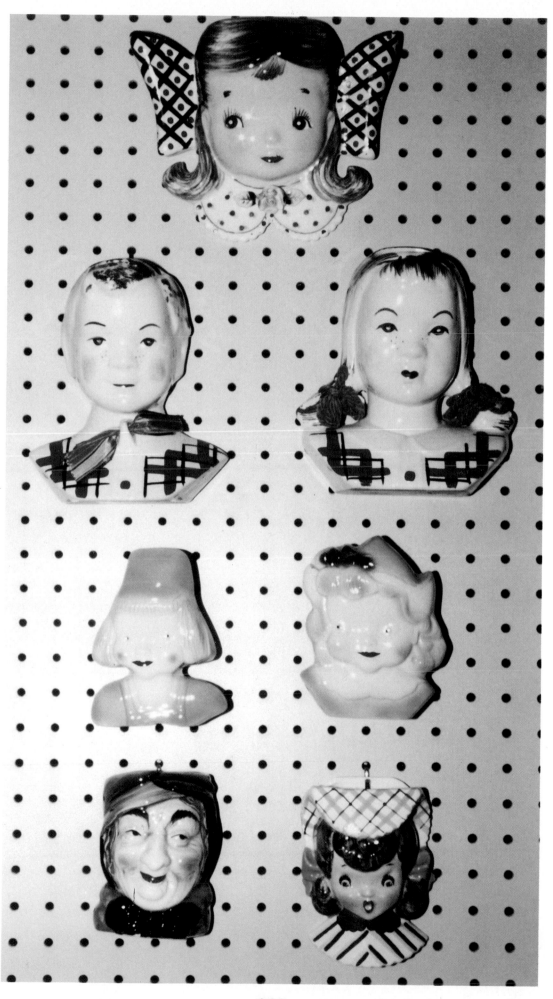

Shawnee Pottery Company

Shawnee Pottery Company operated from 1937 through 1961, in Zanesville, Ohio, producing inexpensive art ware, vases, flower pots and figurines, as well as some very collectable cookie jars and salt and pepper shakers. Just as collectable are their wall pockets. Shawnee made some very high quality pottery. The only complaint we have is that they did not mark a lot of it, which makes it difficult to identify unless you know your Shawnee pottery.

ROW 1:
1. Teapot, mauve fruit, no mark. $20.00 - $25.00

2. Little Bo Peep, mark, "U.S.A. 586." $35.00 - $40.00

3. Little Jack Horner, mark, "U.S.A. 585." $35.00 - $40.00

ROW 2:
1. Teapot, blue fruit, no mark. $20.00 - $25.00

2. Clock, pink and yellow, 20 after 8 o'clock, mark, $30.00 - $35.00
    "U.S.A. 530."

3. Blue birds on bird house, mark "USA." $20.00 - $25.00

ROW 3:
1. Teapot, yellow fruit, no mark. $20.00 - $25.00

2. Mauve color birds, on bird house, no mark. $20.00 - $25.00

3. Blue birds on bird house, no mark. $20.00 - $25.00

ROW 4:
1. Teapot, pink fruit, no mark. $20.00 - $25.00

2. Aqua color birds on bird house with mauve trim, $20.00 - $25.00
    mark, "U.S.A. 830."

3. Mauve color birds on bird house, with aqua trim, $20.00 - $25.00
    mark, "U.S.A. 830."

ROW 5:

Yellow bow, mark, "USA 434." $20.00 - $25.00

U.S.A. Marked

The wall pockets in this chapter are marked only with "U.S.A." A lot of potteries marked their wall pockets with "U.S.A.," and if you know their mold marks, colors and glazes, and do a lot of research, you can identify some of them. We could not identify the pottery(ies) that made the wall pockets listed below.

ROW 1:
1.   Multi-color stove, mark, incised, "U.S.A." $15.00 - $20.00

2.   White bowl with cherries and yellow fork and $15.00 - $20.00
     spoon, mark, incised, "MADE IN USA."

3.   Multi-color stove, mark, incised, "U.S.A."
                                              Price per pair - $32.00 - $42.00

ROW 2:
1.   Green pepper on leaf, mark, incised, "U.S.A." $15.00 - $20.00

2.   Pitcher and bowl, mark, incised, "U.S.A." $15.00 - $20.00

3.   Orange color tulip on leaf, mark, incised, "U.S.A." $20.00 - $25.00

ROW 3:
1.   Hen, mark, incised, "MADE IN USA 916." $30.00 - $35.00

2.   Rooster, mark, incised, "MADE IN USA 915." $25.00 - $30.00

            Hen and rooster price per pair - $60.00 - $75.00

The above pair sit in metal holders for hanging.

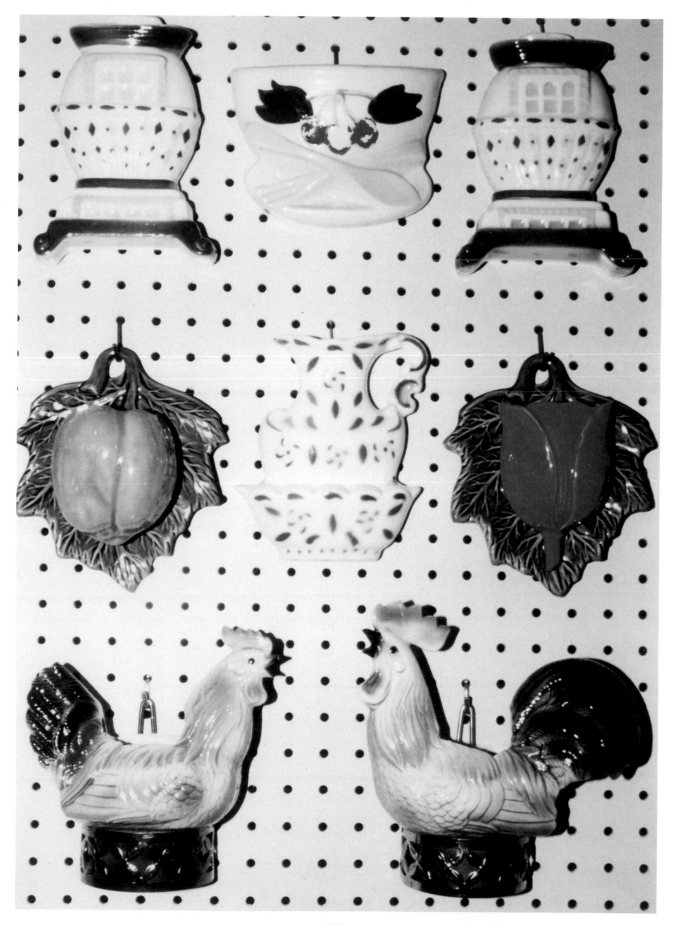

284

U.S.A. Marked

ROW 1:

    1.   White with flowers and blue bow, trimmed with gold, mark, incised, "U.S.A." $15.00 - $20.00

    2.   Hand, mark, incised, "U.S.A." $35.00 - $50.00

    3.   White with flowers and mauve bow, trimmed with gold, mark, incised, "U.S.A." $15.00 - $20.00

ROW 2:

    1.   Lavabo design, gold brocade, mark, in gold letters, "24 KT. GOLD MADE IN U.S.A." $25.00 - $30.00

    2.   Blue and white lamp, trimmed with gold, mark, incised, "U.S.A." $20.00 - $25.00

    3.   Lavabo design, gold brocade, mark, in gold letters, "24 KT. GOLD MADE IN U.S.A."

        Price per pair - $55.00 - $65.00

ROW 3:

    1.   Brown flower, mark, incised, "U.S.A." $10.00 - $15.00

    2.   Pitcher and bowl, gold brocade, mark, in gold letters, "24 KT. GOLD MADE IN U.S.A." $25.00 - $30.00

    3.   Blue flower, trimmed with gold, mark, incised, "U.S.A." $12.00 - $17.00

U.S.A. Marked

ROW 1:

1. Small green with ivy pattern, mark, incised, "MADE IN USA." $12.00 - $15.00

2. Basket type pattern, aqua blue color, mark, incised, "MADE IN USA." $12.00 - $15.00

3. Small green with ivy pattern, mark, incised, "MADE IN USA." $25.00 - $35.00

ROW 2:

1. Green with vertical lines, mark, incised, "MADE IN USA." $12.00 - $15.00

2. Yellow with vertical lines, mark, incised, "MADE IN USA." $12.00 - $15.00

3. White with vertical lines, mark, incised, "MADE IN USA." $12.00 - $15.00

ROW 3:

1. Large green with ivy pattern, mark, incised, "MADE IN USA." $15.00 - $20.00

2. Basket type pattern, aqua blue color, mark, incised, "MADE IN USA."   Price per pair - $25.00 - $32.00

3. Large green with ivy pattern, mark, incised, "MADE IN USA."   Price per pair - $32.00 - $42.00

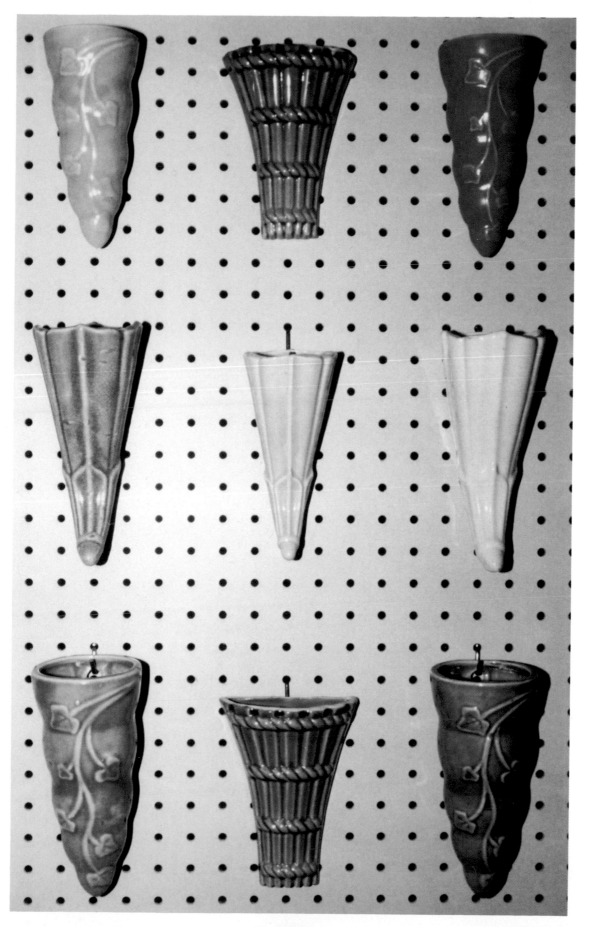

U.S.A. Marked

ROW 1:

    1.   Brown butterfly, mark, incised, "USA." $15.00 - $20.00

    2.   Brown fish, mark, incised, "USA." $15.00 - $20.00

ROW 2:

    1.   Wire hangers with light gray floral design pockets, mark, incised, "826 MADE IN USA." $10.00 - $12.00

    2.   Pink water bottle, mark, incised, "1303 USA." $15.00 - $20.00

    3.   Wire hangers with light gray floral design pockets, mark, incised, "826 MADE IN USA." $22.00 - $25.00

ROW 3:

    1.   Dark brown pair of cowboy boots, marked with paper label, "SOUVENIR OF GARDEN CITY, MO." $10.00 - $12.00

    2.   Wire hanger with tan basket weave design pocket, mark, incised, "827 MADE IN U.S.A." $10.00 - $12.00

    3.   Multi-color brown and green pair of cowboy boots, mark, incised, "USA." $10.00 - $12.00

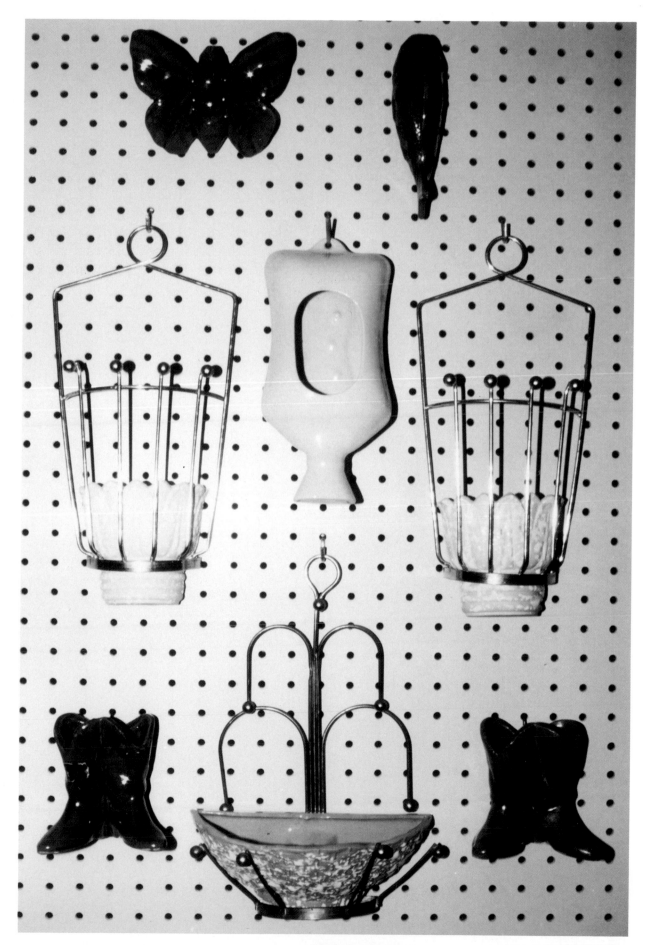

Van Briggle

Van Briggle Pottery started in Colorado Springs, Colorado in 1901, by Artus Van Briggle. His wife, Anne, worked with him until his death in 1904. She continued with their work and the pottery is still in production today. Until the early 1920's, Van Briggle Pottery was marked with the date and design number. Since then they have marked their wares with "AA."

Our source of information is Lois Crouch of Colorado Springs, Colorado. She wrote a book on the early Van Briggle works of Artus and Anne. According to Lois, several types of wall pockets were made from 1922 through 1926. We have only found this one, and have seen pictures of two others.

ROW 1:

Double lily flower design, in ming soft blue color, with dull matte glaze finish. $175.00 - $225.00

Mark, in blue, "2," and incised, "3 - AA Van Briggle COLO SPGS."

Weller

The Weller Pottery Company was started in Zanesville, Ohio in 1882 and continued until 1948. During their years of operation they made many beautiful wall pockets. Many of their wall pockets were not marked. Thanks again to Jerry and Ann McClain of Higginsville, Missouri, for sharing their Weller wall pockets with us.

ROW 1:
1. Warwick, 11 1/2", made in late 1920's, no mark. $125.00 - $150.00

2. Malvern, 11", made in late 1920's, no mark. $125.00 - $175.00

3. Mirror Black, 8 1/2", made in early 1920's, no mark. $125.00 - $150.00

4. Mirror Black, 8 1/2", made in early 1920's, no mark. $125.00 - $150.00

ROW 2:
1. Woodcraft, 9 1/2", made in 1920's through early 1930's, no mark. $125.00 - $150.00

2. Marvo, 7 1/2", made mid 1920's through early 1930's, no mark. $110.00 - $150.00

3. Klyro, 7 1/2", made late 1920's, marked with a Klyro label. $125.00 - $150.00

4. Blue Ware, 10", made early 1900's, mark, incised, "WELLER." $150.00 - $200.00

5. Fairfield, 9 1/2", made 1916 - 1917, no mark. $150.00 - $200.00

Weller

ROW 1:

1. Yellow birds on nest, with cherries, 4 1/2", no mark. $30.00 - $40.00

2. Woodcraft, 11 1/2", mark, incised, "WELLER," made in 1920's. $150.00 - $200.00

3. Red birds on nest, with blue flower 5", no mark. $30.00 - $40.00

ROW 2:

1. Woodrose, 10", made early 1900's, mark, incised, "WELLER." $150.00 - $200.00

2. Woodrose, 6 1/2", made early 1900's, mark, incised, "WELLER." $100.00 - $150.00

3. Woodrose, 5 1/2", made early 1900's, mark, incised, "WELLER." $100.00 - $150.00

ROW 3:

1. Woodrose, 6", made early 1900's, no mark. $65.00 - $100.00

2. Brown birds on nest, 7 1/2", no mark. $40.00 - $45.00

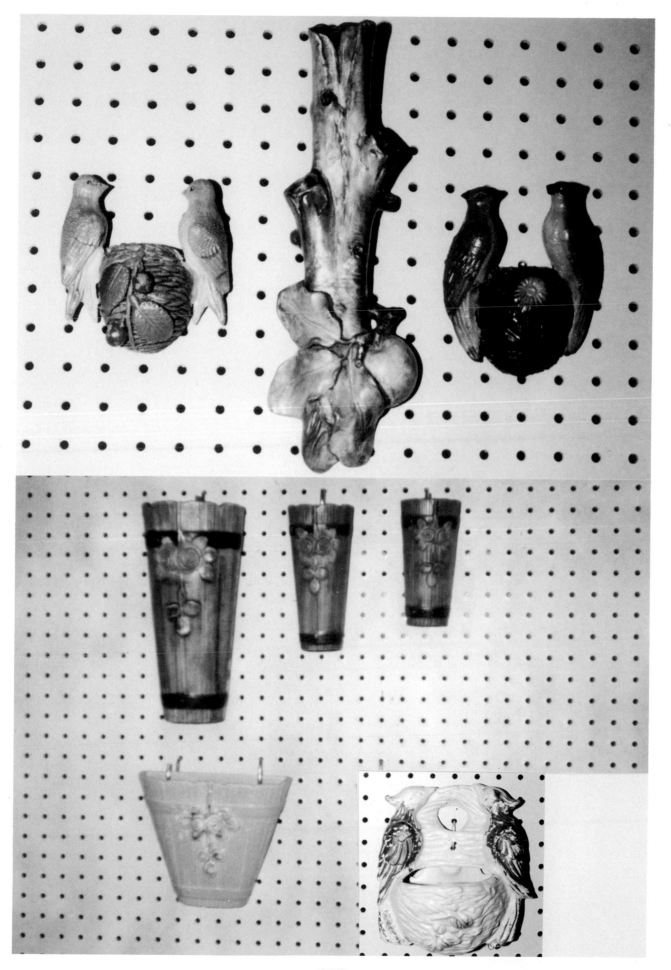

Wood, Plastic, Metal, Chalk
Odds and Ends

The wall pockets in this chapter are an assortment of different types of wall pockets and wall hangings that we feel are an important part of our collection. Wall pockets were originally designed to root plants in, but each of the pockets in this chapter were made to hang on the wall to hold something: matches, wooden toothpicks, letters, artificial flowers, rings and things, so all are included.

ROW 1:

1. Wood scoop, pocket for letters, no mark. $5.00 - $7.00

2. Old tin pocket, painted black with gold roses, also has small mirror. Used for combs and things, no mark. $25.00 - $35.00

ROW 2:

1. Wooden owl pocket, used to hold wooden matches or toothpicks, no mark. $5.00 - $7.00

2. Wooden oriental design, pocket for letters, combs and things, no mark. $25.00 - $35.00

3. Wooden eagle pocket, used to hold wooden matches or toothpicks, no mark. $5.00 - $7.00

ROW 3:

This pair is made of wood, with a gold colored, textured finish, mark in white numbers on back, "No 55."   Price per pair - $15.00 - $20.00

Odds and Ends

ROW 1:

1. Plastic wall pocket, mark, "COPYRIGHT MCMLXXI HOMCO INC., MADE IN U.S.A." $4.00 - $6.00

2. Plastic wall pocket, mark, "COPYRIGHT MCMLXX II HOMCO INC., 6060 MADE IN U.S.A." $8.00 - $10.00

3. Plastic wall pocket, mark, "COPYRIGHT MCMLXXI HOMCO INC., MADE IN U.S.A."
   Price per pair - $8.00 - $12.00

ROW 2:

1. Large metal pocket, gold color, no mark. $8.00 - $10.00

2. Medium metal pocket, gold color, no mark. $6.00 - $8.00

3. Small metal pocket, gold color, no mark. $4.00 - $6.00
   Price per pair - $20.00 - $25.00

ROW 3:

1. Plastic cornucopia, gold color, no mark. $3.00 - $5.00

2. Brass metal pocket, soldered joints, will hold water, no mark. $6.00 - $8.00

3. Plastic cornucopia, gold color, no mark.
   Price per pair - $7.00 - $10.00

ROW 4:

1. Wooden pocket, match holder, mark on front, "Marcell, Minn." $4.00 - $6.00

2. Wooden pocket, holds two pencils, mark on front, "VICTORIA B.C. CANADA." $5.00 - $8.00

3. Plastic pitcher wall pocket, gold color, no mark. $3.00 - $5.00

Odds and Ends

ROW 1:
1. Dull clay pocket, hand made, has leaf design in black, mark, incised, "Floyd ©." $5.00 - $10.00

2. Glazed clay pocket, hand made, has thumb print design on edge, no mark. $5.00 - $7.00

ROW 2:
1. Long match pocket, clay, hand made, yellow flower design, no mark. $10.00 - $12.00

2. Round clay pocket, hand made, has flower and thumb print design, mark, incised, "TN 9-2-79." $12.00 - $15.00

3. Clay pocket, little girl face with big hat, hand made, no mark. $12.00 - $15.00

ROW 3:
1. Dark brown glazed clay pocket, hand made, has spiral design, mark, incised, "Hogenson 77." $5.00 - $7.00

2. Glazed clay pocket, hand made, yellow, brown and red colors, no mark. $5.00 - $7.00

3. Dark brown glazed clay pocket, hand made, has spiral design, mark, incised, "Hogenson 77."
Price per pair - $12.00 - $15.00

ROW 4:
1. Glazed clay with two pockets, gray blue colors, has thumb print design, no mark. $5.00 - $10.00

2. Mexican clay patio pocket, has Mexican design, hand made, has drain hole in bottom, no mark. $10.00 - $12.00

3. Dull clay pocket with leather strap for hanging, hand made, wild flower design, green glaze inside, no mark. $10.00 - $12.00

Odds and Ends

ROW 1:

1. Pottery, pink with flower, mark, incised, "Sleetal 1978." $5.00 - $7.00

2. Girl and boy, in black letters on front, ". . HAPPINESS IS BEING WITH YOU," mark on back, incised, "© 76 BELL CERAMICS MM." $7.00 - $10.00

ROW 2:

1. Plastic brown Dutch shoe, mark, in raised letters, "© JOSEPH MARKOVITS INC. 1970." $3.00 - $5.00

2. Plastic white and red gym shoe, mark, in raised letters, "B 3221 © BURWOOD PRODUCTS CO. MCMXICI MADE IN USA." $10.00 - $12.00

3. Plastic brown Dutch shoe, mark, in raised letters, no mark.   Price per pair - $7.00 - $10.00

ROW 3:

1. Plastic hobnail vase, no mark. $3.00 - $5.00

2. Plastic lady's hat with pink ribbon and white daisies, mark in raised letters, "2705-1-2 © BURWOOD PROD. CO. MCMLXXV MADE IN USA." $8.00 - $10.00

3. Plastic hobnail vase, no mark. Price per pair - $7.00 - $10.00

ROW 4:

1. Pottery, white with plaid design, rope hangers, mark, in raised letters, "(DEER) KERAMICK 292." $8.00 - $10.00

2. Pottery, white with coffee pot, pans, and in black, "POTHOLDERS," no mark. $10.00 - $12.00

3. Pottery, white with plaid design, rope hangers, mark, in raised letters, "(DEER) KERAMICK 292."   Price per pair - $17.00 - $21.00

Odds and Ends

ROW 1:
1. Metal bellows with rooster design, brass color, mark, in raised numbers, "7412." $10.00 - $12.00

2. Ruby red glass rooter, hanging in white wire holder, no mark. $7.00 - $10.00

3. Tin cup, no mark. $5.00 - $7.00

ROW 2:
1. Black metal fork, mark, incised, "© SEXTON USA 1969-1209." $8.00 - $12.00

2. Ruby red glass rooter, hanging in black wire holder, with metal tulip on top, no mark. $7.00 - $10.00

3. Ruby red glass rooter, hanging in black wire holder, with metal tulip on top, no mark.
Price per pair - $15.00 - $25.00

4. Black metal spoon, mark, incised, "© SEXTON USA 1969-12009." $8.00 - $12.00
Price per pair - $20.00 - $25.00

ROW 3:
1. Copper color plastic pitcher, mark, in raised letters, "COPYRIGHT MCMLXXXIII, HOMCO INC, MADE IN USA 7649 E." $4.00 - $6.00

2. Green pottery top and pocket, in a black wire holder, no mark. $10.00 - $15.00

3. Heavy cast metal pot with handles, silver color, no mark. $10.00 - $15.00

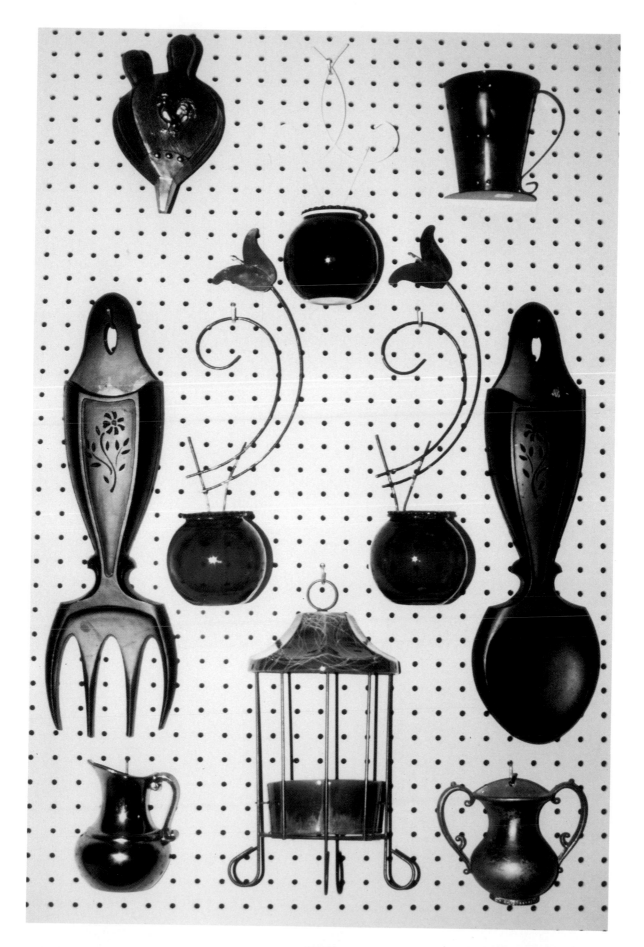

Odds and Ends

ROW 1:

1.   Plastic lady's white hat with pink ribbon and $8.00 - $10.00
flowers, no mark.

2.   Pottery with lady holding flowers, pink color, mark, $20.00 - $25.00
paper label, "HALLMARK-HALLMARK, CARDS, INC.,
K.C., MO 64141 MADE IN TAIWAN WHD 1221."
Original price tag on back $20.00.

ROW 2:

1.   Pottery lavabo, two pieces, light gray color, birds $25.00 - $30.00
and floral design, mark, paper label, "ARDCO
FINE QUALITY DALLAS, MADE IN JAPAN."

2.   Pottery lavabo, two pieces, aqua color, deco design $15.00 - $20.00
with grape trim, no mark.

ROW 3:

1.   Pottery, green butterfly, mark, paper label, "MADE $5.00 - $7.00
IN TAIWAN R.O.C." Original price tag on back
$5.99.

2.   Pottery, white dove of peace, has olive branch in $10.00 - $15.00
beak, mark, incised, "© 1992 HOUSE OF LLOYD."

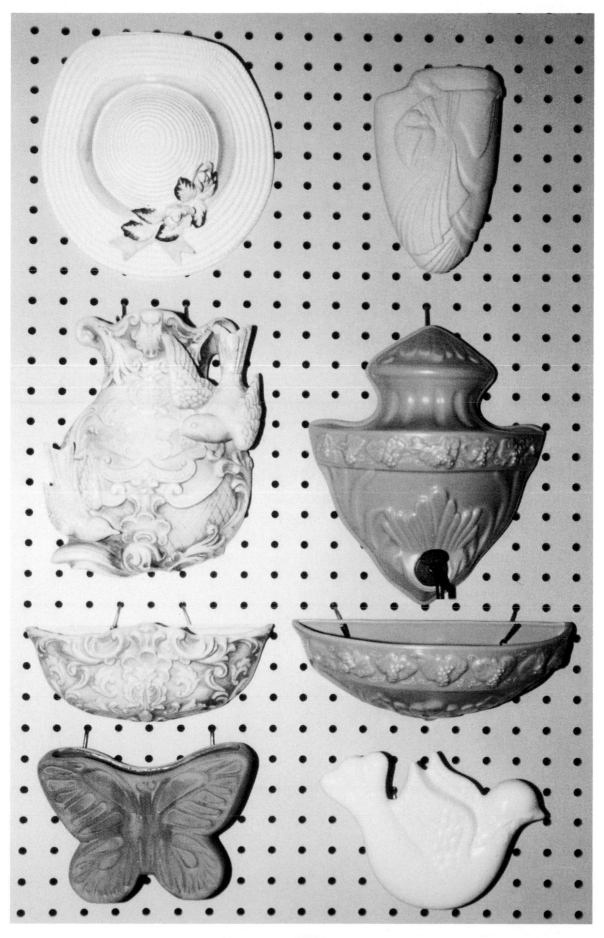

Odds and Ends

The hanging pocket baskets are very pretty and originally hung on chains made of porcelain. Of course, the chains have become lost or broken over the years and are difficult to find.

ROW 1:

1. Pottery hanging basket, blue with tree, sun and bird, mark, incised, "MADE IN JAPAN." $30.00 - $35.00

2. Pottery hanging basket, brown with tree and bird, mark, incised, "MADE IN JAPAN." $30.00 - $35.00

ROW 2:

Hanging basket made of cloisonne over porcelain, black color, owl has rhinestones for eyes. Also has hole for hanging, mark, incised, "MADE IN JAPAN." $35.00 - $40.00

ROW 3:

1. Pottery hanging basket, green with multi-color flowers, mark, in red letters, "MADE IN JAPAN." $25.00 - $30.00

2. Pottery hanging basket, yellow with fruit, mark, in black letters, "MADE IN JAPAN." $30.00 - $35.00

ROW 4:

Pottery planter or hanging pocket, because it has a hole in each end for a cord or chain, white with plums, no mark. Looks like Morton Pottery. $30.00 - $40.00

ROW 5:

1. Pottery hanging basket, red with blue parrot, mark, in black letters, "MADE IN JAPAN." $40.00 - $50.00

2. Pottery hanging basket, red with white bird, no mark. $30.00 - $40.00

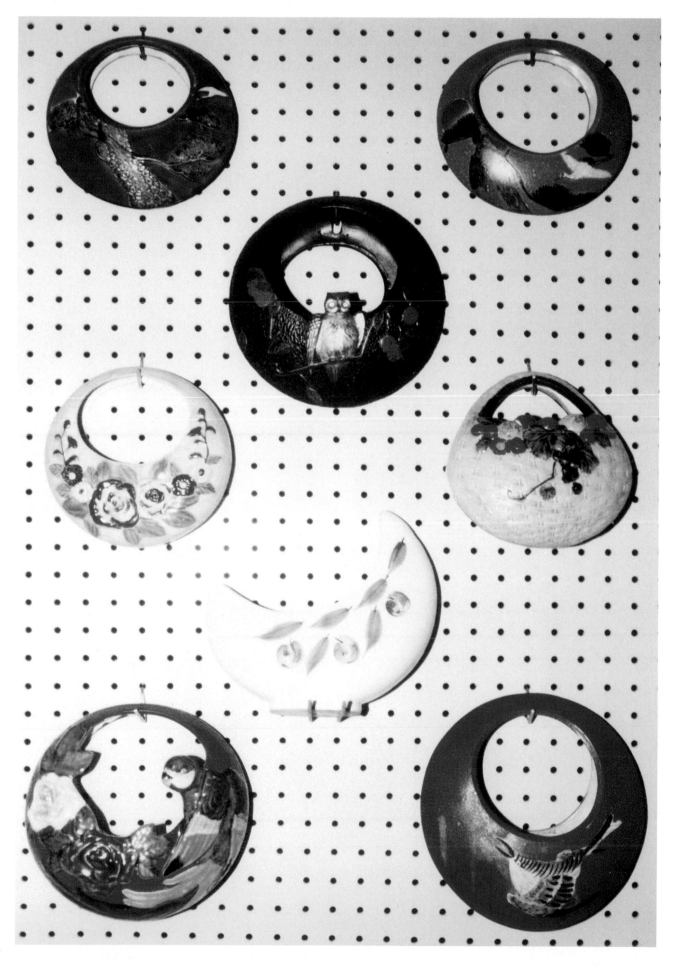

Odds and Ends

The electric lamps on this page are made of pottery and are quite plentiful, once you know how to identify them. We have regular wall pockets just like some of them, so I'm sure they were adapted from them.

ROW 1:
1. Lamp with cord, brown tea kettle, rooster on front, mark, paper label, "Royal Sealy JAPAN." $15.00 - $20.00

2. Lamp with cord, white with pair of birds, mark incised, "©." $20.00 - $30.00

ROW 2:
1. Lamp with cord, chartreuse with green leaves, mark, incised, "Bucking-ham." $20.00 - $30.00

2. Wall pocket, white with red trim and cherries, mark, incised, "299 Stanford Sebring, O." $20.00 - $25.00

3. Lamp with cord, with red trim and cherries, mark, incised, "#299." $20.00 - $30.00

ROW 3:
1. Lamp with cord, with coffee pot with red flowers, no mark. $20.00 - $25.00

2. Wall pocket, white coffee pot with red flowers, no mark. $15.00 - $20.00

3. Lamp with cord, telephone with flowers, no mark. $20.00 - $30.00

ROW 4:
Electric clock, no mark on pottery case. Clock is "SESSIONS, MADE IN U.S.A." $60.00 - $80.00

The clock is the only one we have found. It has a pocket on each side of the clock and will actually hold water.

Odds and Ends

All the birds and hanging pots on this page are made of pottery.

ROW 1:

Pink Cockateel, mark in black letters, "MARUHOM WARE (K) HAND PAINTED JAPAN. . . " $20.00 - $30.00

ROW 2:

1. Red and yellow parrot sitting in wire hanger, back is open for rooting plants, no mark. $35.00 - $40.00

2. Pot with multi-color fruit design, hanging from brass chain, mark, in black letters, "MADE IN JAPAN." $20.00 - $30.00

3. Red and green parrot sitting in wire hanger, back is open for rooting plants, mark, in black numbers, "5168." $30.00 - $40.00

ROW 3:

1. Red parrot with yellow tail, back is open for rooting plants, mark, paper label, "dabs JAPAN." $30.00 - $40.00

2. Pot pocket, red basket weave design with white flowers on black handles, has three holes for hanging, no mark. $20.00 - $30.00

3. Same parrot as #1 in row 2. We took it out of the wire hanger, so you could see the side view, no mark. $35.00 - $40.00

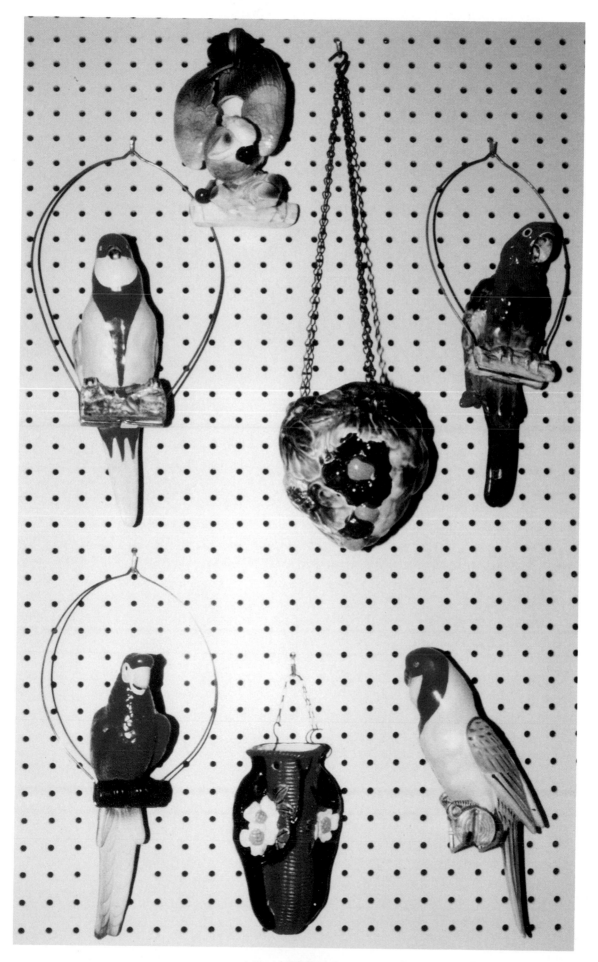

Odds and Ends

ROW 1:
1. Pottery, yellow pitcher for holding four measuring spoons, mark, incised, "PAT. APPLIED FOR." $7.00 - $10.00

2. Pottery yellow and green holds four measuring spoons, mark, incised, "PAT PEND." $10.00 - $12.00

3. Pottery, yellow and green, holds four measuring spoons, mark, incised, "PAT PEND." $10.00 - $12.00

ROW 2:
1. Pottery, little lady stringer, trimmed in green, mark, in red letters, "JAPAN." $25.00 - $30.00

2. Pottery, black mammy stringer in plaid dress, mark, in black letters, "MADE IN JAPAN." $140.00 - $160.00

3. Pottery kitten stringer with pink ball of yarn, mark, in black letters, "JAPAN." $15.00 - $30.00

ROW 3:
1. Pottery match box holder, marked, "Cb CLEMIN-SON'S Hand Painted." $15.00 - $20.00

2. Pottery lady with yellow hat, holds four measuring spoons, no mark. $20.00 - $25.00

3. Pottery stove used to hold matches or toothpicks, no mark. $15.00 - $25.00

ROW 4:
1. Black cast iron match holder, no mark. $15.00 - $20.00

2. Pottery match box holder, also holds toothpicks on each side, no mark. $15.00 - $20.00

3. Plastic holder for note pad and two pencils, on front in black print, "NELSON & CROUCH Painting & Decorating, Phone 319, W. Boone, IA." No mark. $5.00 - $7.00

Odds and Ends

ROW 1:

1. Plastic toothpaste and brush holder, yellow with black cat, no mark. $5.00 - $7.00

2. Pottery what's it?, Full of tiny holes, mark, "53/590 Hand painted TILSO JAPAN." $10.00 - $12.00

3. Plastic toothpaste and brush holder, green with white cat, no mark. $5.00 - $7.00

ROW 2:

1. Pottery toothpaste and brush holder, horse with plaid design, mark, in black letters, "MADE IN JAPAN." $20.00 - $25.00

2. Pottery toothpaste and brush holder, woman dressed in blue, mark, paper label, "ENESCO IMPORTS JAPAN." $15.00 - $20.00

3. Pottery toothpaste and brush holder, orange colored mule, mark, "GOLDCASTLE-CHIKUSA MADE IN JAPAN." $20.00 - $25.00

ROW 3:

1. Pottery rooter, deer on plate, mark, in black letters, "MADE IN JAPAN." $12.00 - $15.00

2. Pottery rooter, white umbrella, mark, paper label, "Beverly CIMINO COLORADO SPRINGS, COLO." $10.00 - $15.00

3. Pottery bank, print on front, "NICKELS," and "a penny SAVED is a penny Earned," mark, paper label, "MADE IN JAPAN." $15.00 - $20.00

ROW 4:

1. Plastic, painted, looks very old, white pitcher with cherries, no mark. $10.00 - $15.00

2. Pottery, green mail box, made to be used as a mail box or as a patio wall planter, because it has drain holes in the bottom. $10.00 - $15.00

Odds and Ends

All cups and saucers on this page are made of plastic.

ROW 1:

1. Red cup and saucer, blue flower on cup. — $5.00 - $10.00

2. Red cup and saucer, red flower on cup. — $5.00 - $10.00

3. Red cup and saucer, yellow flower on cup. — $5.00 - $10.00
   All three above, marked, "PLAS-TEX PT883 MADE IN U.SA."

ROW 2:

1. Yellow cup and saucer, mark, "PLASTIC PRODUCTS CO. HOLLYWOOD, CALIF., MADE IN U.S.A." — $5.00 - $10.00

2. Red cup on chartreuse saucer, mark, "Maherware 1 MADE IN U.S.A." — $4.00 - $7.00

3. Yellow cup and saucer, marked, "PLASTIC PRODUCTS CO. HOLLYWOOD, CALIF., MADE IN U.S.A."   Price per pair - — $12.00 - $22.00

ROW 3:

1. Yellow pear on white plate, mark, "MADE IN U.S.A." — $5.00 - $10.00

2. Blue cup and saucer, mark, "MADE IN U.S.A." — $3.00 - $5.00

3. Red apple on white plate, mark, "MADE IN U.S.A." — $5.00 - $10.00

ROW 4:

1. Red cup and saucer, mark, "MADE IN USA." — $3.00 - $5.00

2. Red cup and saucer, mark, "MADE IN USA."
   Price per pair - — $7.00 - $12.00

3. Yellow cup and saucer, blue flower, mark, "MADE IN U.S.A." — $3.00 - $5.00

4. Yellow cup and saucer, red flower, mark, "MADE IN U.S.A." — $3.00 - $5.00

ROW 5:

1. Blue cup and saucer, with red tulips, mark, "MADE IN U.S.A." Handle on left. — $4.00 - $6.00

2. Blue cup and saucer, with red tulips, mark, "MADE IN U.S.A." Handle on right. — $4.00 - $6.00
   Price per pair - — $10.00 - $15.00

Odds and Ends

ROW 1:
1. Pottery match holder, boy picking grapes, mark, "MADE IN JAPAN." $25.00 - $30.00

2. Plastic font for holy water, mark, "© ART PLASTIC HONG K0NG." $4.00 - $6.00

3. Hand made glass rooter, green, mark, paper label, "Kasper-single-art reine Kandarbelt." $20.00 - $25.00

ROW 2:
1. Pottery match holder, green and gold trim, no mark. $30.00 - $35.00

2. Pottery soap pad dish, no mark. $7.00 - $10.00

3. Pottery holder for rings and things, mark, "MADE IN TAIWAN." $3.00 - $5.00

ROW 3:
1. Pottery, pink flowers, no mark. $3.00 - $5.00

2. Pottery, pink flowers, mark, paper label, "MADE IN TAIWAN." $3.00 - $5.00

3. Pottery, pink flowers, mark, paper label, "MADE IN TAIWAN." $3.00 - $5.00

   The above three are marked on front in black letters, "Rings and Things."

4. Pottery ring holder, white with oranges, on front, "FLORIDA." $3.00 - $5.00

ROW 4:
1. Pottery alarm clock ring holder, white with pink roses, on front in black letters, "Rings and Things," mark, in red letters, "TAIWAN." $3.00 - $5.00

2. Brass metal holder, no mark. $10.00 - $15.00

3. Pottery alarm clock ring holder, white with pink roses, on front in black letters, "Rings and Things," mark, in blue letters, "TAIWAN." $3.00 - $5.00

Odds and Ends

All of the above silhouette wall hangings on this page are made of plastic. All have plastic pockets to be used as rooters. They were popular during the 1940's thru the 1950's.

ROW 1:
    1.   Silhouette of pot with handles, black and pink colors, no mark. $5.00 - $10.00

    2.   Silhouette of Dutch boy carrying pots, black and white colors, no mark. $10.00 - $15.00

ROW 2:
    1.   Silhouette of man riding an old high wheel bike, black and white colors. The pocket is white with a black ivy design on it, no mark. $10.00 - $15.00

    2.   Silhouette of lady at spinning wheel, black and yellow colors. The pocket is yellow with black ivy design, no mark. $10.00 - $15.00

ROW 3:
    1.   Silhouette of girl watering flowers, red with yellow pocket, marked with raised letters, "U.S. DESIGN PATENT No. 161,230." $10.00 - $15.00

    2.   Silhouette of white flying ducks with cattails in background, black and white colors, no mark. $10.00 - $15.00

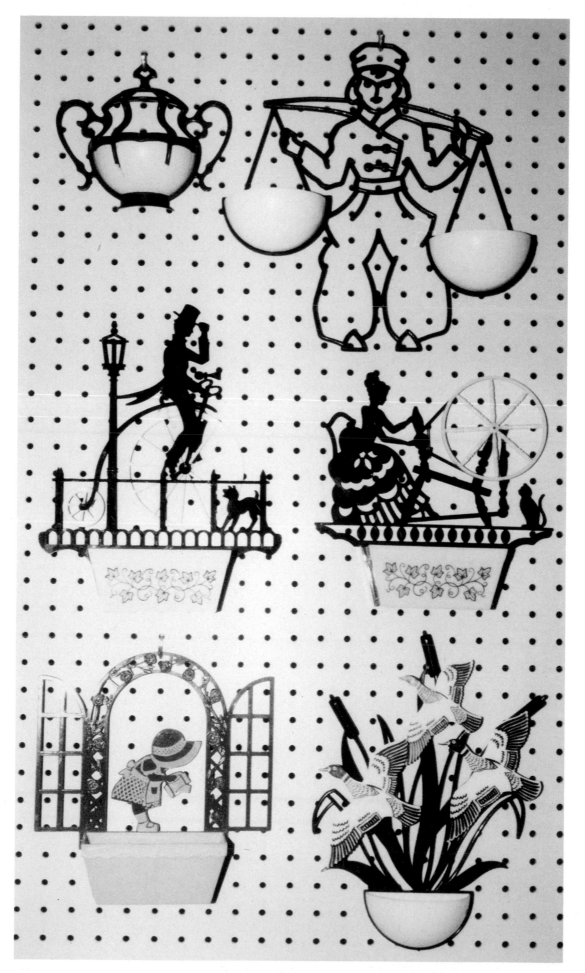

324

Odds and Ends

All wall pockets on this page are made of pottery and are used to hold scissors. Most of all have the same verse printed on the front, as follows:

"I Keep my
SCISSORS
In This Rack . . .
If You Use Them
Please Put Them
BACK!"

ROW 1:
1. White, toad and flower, no mark. $5.00 - $8.00

2. Red, verse in gold print, no mark. $5.00 - $10.00

3. Yellow, printed on front, "SHEARS," mark, "Hand $10.00 - $12.00
    Decorated Made In Calif."

ROW 2:
1. White with flowers and blue trim, verse in gold $5.00 - $10.00
    print, no mark.

2. Pink with flowers, verse in black print, no mark. $5.00 - $10.00

3. Blue flowers and trim, verse in black print, no $5.00 - $10.00
    mark.

ROW 3:
1. Tan, brown trim, pink flowers, verse in gold print, $7.00 - $12.00
    mark, incised, "WFH 616186."

2. Yellow roses, verse in gold print, mark, incised, $7.00 - $12.00
    "CF."

3. Tan with toadstools, no mark. $5.00 - $10.00

ROW 4:
1. White with toadstools and yellow trim, verse in $7.00 - $12.00
    gold print, no mark.

2. White with flowers and gold trim, verse in gold $7.00 - $12.00
    print, no mark.

3. Light pink with flowers, verse in gold print, no $7.00 - $12.00
    mark.

326

Odds and Ends

All wall pockets on this page are made of pottery. These were popular in the 1940's through 1950's. They were made to hang on the wall in the bathroom. The tank was open to hold a pack of cigarettes, and the front was used as an ashtray. For an example, look at #3 in row 3. This was a wall pocket made for the smoker.

ROW 1:

1. Pink toilet with gold trim, no mark. $5.00 - $7.00

2. Hillbilly on stool, print on front, "PUT YOUR HOT $7.00 - $12.00
   BUTT HERE," mark, paper label, "JAPAN."

3. Blue toilet with gold trim, paper label on front - $5.00 - $7.00
   "LITTLE JOHN
   A CIGARETTE SET
   To complete your bathroom and add
   to your comfort."

ROW 2:

1. Pink toilet with gold trim, has "LITTLE JOHN" $5.00 - $7.00
   label on front, mark, paper label, "MADE IN
   JAPAN."

2. Hillbilly with feet in stool, print on front, "HILL- $7.00 - $12.00
   BILLY FOOT BATH," no mark.

3. Pink toilet with "LITTLE JOHN" label on front, no $5.00 - $7.00
   mark.

ROW 3:

1. Man wearing hat trying to flush himself down toilet, $7.00 - $12.00
   print on seat, "GOODBYE CRUEL WORLD," and
   mark, paper label, "MADE IN JAPAN."

2. Toilet with flowers, print on seat, "REST YOUR $5.00 - $10.00
   TIRED ASH," and mark, "St. Pierre & Patterson
   1954."

3. Toilet with flowers and print on seat, "BEST SEAT $5.00 - $10.00
   IN THE HOUSE." Has a pack of cigarettes in holder,
   and a cigarette in the ashtray, no mark.

Odds and Ends

All wall pockets on this page are made of chalk, which is made from plaster of paris, and then painted. Collectors usually refer to it as chalkware. The wall pockets were not intended to be used for rooting plants, but were made as an ornamental piece to be hung on the wall for decoration. They were an inexpensive item when sold, and a lot of them were given away as prizes at carnival games, which is why they are sometimes referred to as carnival pieces. They were made in the U.S.A. from around 1900 up to the 1940's. The history of chalkware goes back to Europe into the 1800's.

ROW 1:
1. Green parrot with yellow pockets on each side, used to hold matches and/or toothpicks, no mark. $15.00 - $20.00

2. Yellow lemon used to hold matches and/or tooth picks, mark, incised, "©." $10.00 - $15.00

ROW 2:
1. Blue basket with bow and flowers, no mark. $15.00 - $20.00

2. Yellow basket with bow and flowers, no mark. $15.00 - $20.00

ROW 3:
1. Brown with pink roses, no mark. $7.00 - $10.00

2. Yellow with red headed green parrot, no mark. $25.00 - $30.00

3. Brown with pink roses, no mark. $15.00 - $20.00

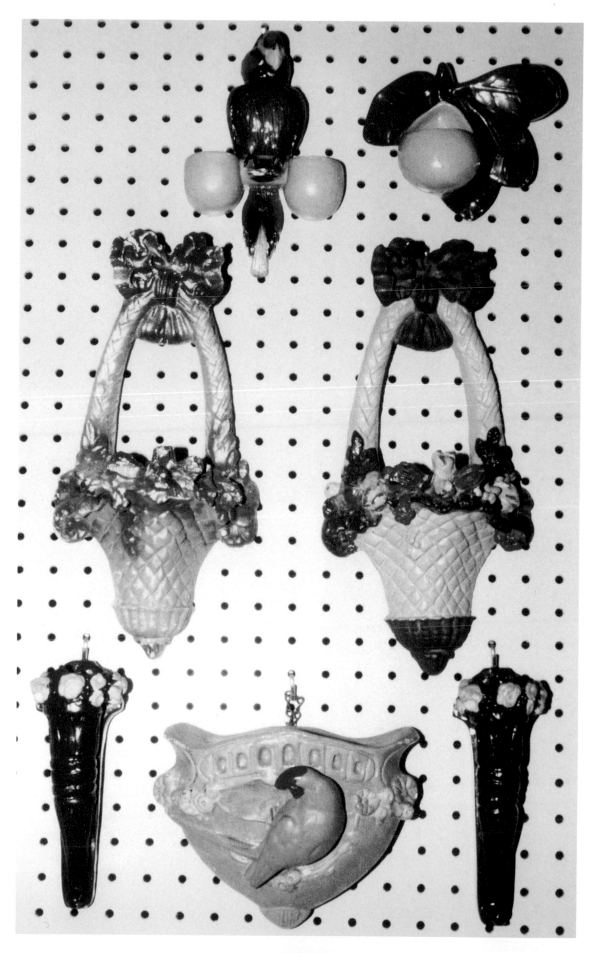